3 Words for Ge
Live Ye:

by Travis L. Thomas

For Hollister and the Purposettes!

Table of Contents

Introduction

Gina wakes up without a desire to get out of bed. The thought of going through the same routine, doing the same uninspired work, and then returning home to do it all over again paralyzes her.

Something has to change, but what?

All she can think is that there must be more to life than this.

*   *   *

Wren never saw the diagnosis coming. There is never a *good* time to get cancer, but this timing couldn't be worse. Newly married, a baby on the way, and the start of an exciting career has just taken a backseat to this tragic news.

He doesn't have time for this. Denial is his only response. All he can think is this can't be happening. Not him. Not now.

He stumbles forward while stuck in the question, "Why me?"

*   *   *

Trent has landed his dream job, but now is where the challenge begins. Change and transition is never easy, especially when you are the new guy in charge of unifying a company of underperforming employees. He is filled with passion and new ideas, but the degrees on his wall aren't enough for this challenge.

He wants to make a difference. He wants to improve the culture. But, where in the heck does he start?

*   *   *

April has only known one life for the past 40 years. A wife, mother, grandmother, and consistent volunteer in her community. She likes her life. It's comfortable, familiar, and filled with meaning. She wasn't anticipating the betrayal and subsequent divorce. In an instant her life has been flipped upside down.

She needs to adapt, but she doesn't want to. She needs to move forward, but she can only look back. She is searching for answers, but only finding more questions.

She craves peace. She wants to be free. But the reality is…

She is stuck!

*   *   *

And then there is you! Your life. Your story. Odds are as you read through the experiences of the people above you made a connection. Something resonated. You have been there.

You may even feel stuck in your life right now.

We all get stuck. Whether it is a relationship, job, our health, our home, or not knowing how to pursue the goals and dreams we have in our hearts.

We're stuck!

If you are able to relate to any of this than I am confident you will find value in the pages that follow.

I have been stuck before (up to my neck in quicksand stuck). I have been stuck while writing this book. I will get stuck again. But I know that my stuck-i-ness is not rare to me. We all get stuck. It's what we *do* when we get stuck that matters. I am here to help.

This is my story.

For over the past 10 years there has been a bubbling happening inside my heart. I knew there was a message that wanted to come out, but whenever I sat down to articulate it nothing felt right.

Looking back now I realize that with any great idea there needs to be time. The seeds had been planted long ago, yet when I was hoping to see fruits, what was growing instead were the unseen roots.

A few decades have passed since the original seeds were planted, and I am grateful for the garden of inspiration that has patiently and authentically taken root over time.

This book is a collection of my life stories and anecdotes based on adopting these three simple words..."**Live Yes, and**" - and how they are the key to helping us get *unstuck* from any situation life throws our way.

I am not alone. Along the way I have been blessed to befriend and meet others from many walks of life who have embraced and overcome challenges bigger than my own.

Although their stories are exceptional, they are no different than yours. I sought them out (and many times they sought me out) because at the essence of their journey is the spirit of living "yes, and!"

Simple? Yes!

Easy? No.

Yet, that seems to be the way it is for most things in life, and "living yes, and" is no different.

I firmly believe that the best way to find success and happiness is this simple formula:

Passion + Effort = Success

Find the thing that gets you excited to get out of bed in the morning, and then perfect it as your craft. Turn your passion into your profession.

We all have a mission - and "Live Yes, And" is mine!

It has inspired me to stand, deliver, and share its power to thousands of people, and now I hope this book will allow me to spread it even more.

I did not invent the concept of "yes, and" (more on that later), but I have allowed it to sink into my marrow, blend with my DNA, and infiltrate into every aspect of my life. In the process I feel I have found a way to teach and share "Live Yes, And" with philosophical and spiritual depth, and with day-to-day practicality that we all can relate to.

Over the years of living these three words, a number of key principles kept showing up and becoming more clear. I tried to condense these 10 principles into a smaller list, but I couldn't. Each is as important than the other, and each has the potential to transform your life. As you read through the chapters undoubtedly some principles will resonate with you more than others. This is not an "all or nothing" approach to living life. Take what works for you, and discard the rest.

Any of these principles can get you unstuck.

This book is dedicated to you and the life you want to live. The stories in the following pages are intended to get you out of your seat, and onto your path of purpose and potential.

The stuck stops here!

Chapter 1:

The Answer to HOW is YES!

The answer to "how" is "yes!" —Peter Block

It was one of those moments that is forever etched in my mind. It was October in 1998 and my wife and I had just moved to Boston with new jobs.

On our first weekend in town we decided to catch a show in Boston's North End at an improv theater that had opened just a few months earlier.

From the moment those lights went up I was hooked.

This is it! This is what I want to do!

How do I do this?

Growing up I was a cheese ball. As soon as my parents bought a video camera I used it to make horrible home movies with my friends. From hokey horror movies to recreating the NBA Slam-Dunk Contest on our Nerf hoops, to our version of COPS. We thought we were clever.

We weren't.

Regardless, I loved being in front of the camera and creating stories. At a young age I would stay up late enough to watch *Saturday Night Live* and memorize Eddie Murphy and Billy Crystal's sketches even though I didn't understand most of the humor.

It didn't matter. In my mind I thought I was hilarious. My first impression as a child was trying to imitate Robin Leach from *Lifestyles of the Rich and Famous.* To this day I still can't do accents. Just ask my improv partners.

As the youngest in the family my siblings and cousins had to endure my constant need to entertain. It was a pathetic plea for approval. My poor older brother Tiger (not the golfer), was constantly barraged with his little annoying brother and his awful comedy.

"Tiger…Tiger…Tiger…Tig…Tig…Tig…Tig…Tiger… Tiger…"

After a minute or two of effectively tuning me out he would eventually have to give in.

"What!?"

(In my best Billy Crystal butchered impression) "You look mah-velous!"

Yup, imagine that being your life for about 12 years.

It was at this time the seeds of comedy were planted. My dream was to someday be on *Saturday Night Live,* yet pursuing acting or drama classes never occurred to me or my parents. (This is the part of my life where I blame my parents for my professional failures. It's clearly their fault.)

Sports were my real passion as a child, and I definitely wasn't one of those weird "theater" kids. So, if I were ever going to make it into the world of comedy, it wouldn't be by taking the traditional route.

And then there I was in Boston in 1998, and the curtain lifted on the one thing I always wanted to do, but never found the time to actually do.

It was time.

The following Monday I called to sign-up for the Level I class in the *Improv Asylum Training Center.* I was in!

As luck would have it, it was the first training center class for the newly opened theater. This meant getting to work and learn from the three co-owners of the theater who also happened to be performers in the Main Stage cast. These were the performers from the show, and now I was getting to learn from them firsthand.

All it took was one class. That's it. I was all in!

I still remember riding the subway back from the first night and just feeling lit up. It's all I wanted to do. How was I going to survive with only one class a week?

I had an improv addiction!

The next day my wife and I were walking to lunch. I remember this conversation so vividly, the image is still stuck in my head today. We were on Belvidere Street in Boston's Back Bay just about to enter the Prudential Building when I told her, "I am eventually going to make it on to the Main Stage cast."

There was no real reason for my confidence. I was never the bold confident type who would make brash predictions and then back them up. And remember, I had no acting or comedy experience up to this point.

But this was different. There was power and providence behind this feeling. I didn't know "how" I was going to progress to that level and then actually get cast into the show, but a feeling is a feeling.

Have you ever had one of those feelings?

Knowing "how" was unimportant. It was the fact that I knew I needed to be an improviser, so the "how" would just have to take care of itself. Little did I know how profound and prophetic that realization would be in my life. It wasn't until years later that I was introduced to the idea and book by Peter Block titled *"The Answer to HOW is YES!"*

That title sums it up. I didn't know how I was going to fulfill my dream, but all I needed to say in that moment was "yes!"

By saying "yes," I was giving myself permission to move forward in the direction I wanted to go. If I had pulled back and spent too much time in the "how," I would have stopped.

Paralysis from analysis.

When we hang out in the "how" we find all of the "realistic" and "rational" reasons for why it is NOT going to happen.

If I were to stop and entertain those ideas I probably could have come up with this list:

- You're 25 and have never taken an acting or comedy class before.
- Do you actually think you are funny? Based on what?
- You have a new job in a big city and don't have time for this.
- This city has lots of talented actors who actually have experience.
- It's a small cast, and you are 1 in a 1,000.

• Did I mention you are not that funny?

So yes, my list may have looked something like that.

But that didn't matter. I loved it. I couldn't personally control whether I made it to the Main Stage cast or not, but I needed to give it a shot.

Over the next two years I completed all six levels of the training center (In chapters to come I'll share some of the details and learning insights that occurred during this time). Upon completion of the training center the theater was growing so successfully that they needed to develop a second cast to help with touring and corporate shows. After enduring my first-ever professional audition, I am proud to say I was cast as a member of the first ever *Improv Asylum Touring Company.*

A few years later with more transition I became a member of the first ever *Improv Asylum N.E.T. Cast* - a developmental cast to the Main Stage cast.

Not along after that an amazing thing happened. I was called in, sat in front of the owners, and asked if I wanted to join the Main Stage cast.

"Yes!!!!!!!!!"

Three years previous I was walking down Belvidere Street with my wife when I told her I would one day be on the Main Stage. I had a dream without a plan. I knew what I wanted to do but I didn't know "how" it was going to happen. Instead of quitting before even getting started I simply said "yes!"

The answer to HOW is YES.

This book is not about predictions.

It is about the power and possibility that go to work when you say "yes" to what is happening, and then make a decision to be true to yourself, your purpose, and your authenticity.

My experience in Boston proved to me what is possible when you give yourself permission to say "yes," despite the odds, fears, and distractions masked in the "how."

It is obvious to me now that the improv stage was the perfect classroom for being introduced to the power of "yes!" On that street in Boston I took a stand for a dream I believed in, simply by saying "yes." Little did I know that one simple word packed in it the power to change my life, and many more to come.

The answer to HOW is YES.

What that really means is…*the answer to "how" is giving your consent.* Your "yes" is you giving your consent that what you really desire and envision is indeed possible. It might not feel probable, but it doesn't mean it's impossible. Your "yes" is your faith. Your "yes" is your belief.

Most of us stop because we cannot fathom or figure out how something could actually work out. We overthink the situation and convince ourselves that it is hopeless and impossible. We mistake not knowing the "how" as reason for not even beginning in the first place. Our rational and realistic thinking kicks in and dashes our hope, convincing us to stay put, play it safe, and keeping our heads out of the clouds.

Our culture loves focusing on the "how" before there has even been time to consider the possibilities of our dreams. Maybe it was a teacher who discouraged you in grade school, or a parent who didn't want to see you suffer. Or, it is your own nurtured insecurity that doesn't allow you to even entertain such notions. Whatever the reason, society has great aim when it comes to shooting down dreams.

But…

When you say "yes" you embrace the unknown. When you say "yes" you allow forces that you cannot see go to work in your favor. When you say "yes" you step outside of your comfort zone and into your growth zone. Wayne Gretzky once said, "You miss 100% of the shots you don't take."

Your "yes" is where your life begins!

So, now that we have introduced you to the "yes," let's see what is possible when we add the "and."

UN*STUCK* Principle #1:

The Answer to "How" is "Yes!"

Chapter 2:

Life is the Performance!

All the world's a stage... —William Shakespeare

Don't be mislead. This book is not about improvisation.

Well, it is, but not in the comedic way. The focus of this book is not to turn you into a comedic performer on stage, or help you get on *Whose Line Is It Anyway?*

I mean. It can help. But it is not a "how-to" for the aspiring improviser. (If so, I would really be limiting my audience.)

This is not a book about comedy, improv, and theater, but it has everything to do with your performance in life.

All the world's a stage...

My most recent work was as a leadership specialist at the IMG Academy in Florida. IMG Academy is arguably the top athletic training facility in the world. It was started by tennis guru Nick Bollettieri in the late 1970's and gained fame for producing the likes of Andre Agassi, Monica Seles, Jim Courier, and most recently Maria Sharapova and Kei Nishikori. Look at a list of tennis royalty and you can bet they called IMG home for a portion of their professional development.

In the late 80's IMG (International Management Group) purchased the tennis academy and began expanding and adding sports. In 2013, IMG was purchased by WME (William Morris Endeavor) paving the way for even bigger things for the Academy and its professional training.

Step on campus today, and Nick Bollettieri can still be found working with the world's top tennis prospects, but these days they may be sharing the weight room with college football and basketball players preparing for the NFL and NBA combines, elite track and field athletes from all over the world training for the Olympics, MLB players preparing for Spring Training, professional soccer players gearing up for the World Cup, and nearly 1,000 aspiring youth athletes from around the world going to school on campus and training in their sport.

Working at IMG Academy was like living in an ESPN commercial.

Da nah nah - da nah nah!

So, why was an improvisational actor working with professional athletes?

I'll get there, but not yet!

We need to go back to the *Improv Asylum* basement theater where a new relationship was created. It was during those first weeks in the training center that I was introduced to the idea and concept that would transform my life.

Those two words: *yes, and.*

As I mentioned in my introduction, I didn't come up with this "yes, and" concept. In fact, it is hard to pin down who exactly did. Improvisation itself can be tracked back all the way to farce theater in Ancient Rome, which if I do my calculations correctly is roughly a few years before my time.

The important thing is, this concept of "yes, and" is the foundation and cornerstone of improvisation. I cannot find who should be credited with coining the term. If you are out there, I would like to say…

Thank you. You nailed it!

Moving on.

Let's do a little improvisation "Yes, And" 101.

YES = Acceptance of the offer.

In improvisation, an offer is when a performer shares any idea or information, most often in a line of dialogue. Any information shared is considered an offer. An actor walking on stage stomping his feet is an offer, as is the simple line, "It sure is a beautiful day!"

If I am doing a scene with you, and you say, "Travis, you are so handsome!"

That is easy for me to say "yes" to. Saying "yes," I am acknowledging your offer as being real and true in our scene.

If I say "no" to your offer, I am negating your idea, and essentially telling you that as a fellow actor I do not like your idea, or I feel I have a better one.

In the world of improvisation, saying "no" to an offer is a scene killer. It is also a way to guarantee no one wanting to perform with you.

By saying "yes" I confirm that we are on the same page and are working together. It doesn't matter what you say to me, rational or irrational, my only job as an improviser in that moment is to say "yes."

Your offer might be, "Travis, you are the most grotesque man alive!"

Now, as a person, my ego might want to disagree with this offer and come back with a "no!" And odds are my counteroffer would be in the realm of, "No I'm not! You're uglier!"

Sounds like a great scene, huh? So, instead of being in agreement with one another we have simply begun an argument. Arguments often turn into brutally painful train wrecks, although not as fun to watch.

Instead, this scene is going to be much more entertaining for the performers and the audience if I choose to say "yes."

Saying yes puts us both on the same page.

AND = Adding new information to the offer.

The "yes" is about acceptance. The "and" is about building.

Simply put, it is about cooperation instead of competition.

So, in response to "Travis, you are the most grotesque man alive!" Here are a couple of the endless responses that are possible by saying "yes, and":

Yes, and I have held that title for the past 5 years.

Yes, and that is an interesting first wedding vow.

Yes, and I was raised in the wild.

Yes, and I suppose you are not giving me a rose?

Yes, and I am suing my plastic surgeon.

The "and" is adding new information based on the first offer. It is not just good enough to say "yes." You are an active and equal participant in a scene that is being conceived in real time with no script. The "and" is your building idea based on their offer. There is no excuse to not add an idea because there is no wrong idea. Remember, this is improvisation so there are no scripts, and therefore no wrong answers.

That is the power of "yes, and." People often mistake the agreement of saying "yes" with not being able to have conflict. But just because you are in agreement with someone or something doesn't mean you have to like it. (Don't worry, this will be covered later.)

Every great improvised scene has conflict, but the conflict comes from the story, not from the disagreeing performers.

Let me take one of the responses above and play it out how it could happen on stage. It is important to note that with each "yes, and" response, you are responding to the newest idea, not the idea that began the scene. It doesn't mean you disregard what has been established, but your job as an improviser is to respond to the offer you have just been given.

Here is an example:

Performer 1: *"Travis, you are the most grotesque man alive!"*

Performer 2: *"Yes, and that is an interesting first wedding vow."*

Performer 1: *"Yes, and I just want people to know that I am not marrying you for your looks."*

Performer 2: *"Yes, and you made that clear when you booked separate honeymoons."*

Performer 1: *"Yes, and when your brother asked me to Hawaii, I couldn't say no."*

Performer 2: *"Yes, he is the good-looking one."*

Performer 1: *"Yes, and I am going to need your credit card."*

As you can see, there is a whole lot of conflict in this scene, yet the performers still adhere to "yes, anding" each others ideas. And notice that every new offer is in response to the newest information.

The scene has total "yes" agreement between both performers, while every "and" adds and builds off the most recent idea.

When you watch two veteran improvisers perform they may not verbally say "yes, and" after every offer, but their responses will still show agreement and building. For beginning improvisers, the habit of having to say "yes, and" reveals how quickly we want to say "no, but" or "yes, but" instead. More on that later.

Another way to think about an improvised scene is like a tennis rally. Back and forth the two players return hits, using different spins, slices, and pace on the ball to alter their shots. At no time does one player add a different ball during the rally, nor do they ignore the current ball and hit a different ball back in return.

Every return hit is an acceptance (*yes*) of the previous hit, while the choice of how they return the ball adds (*and*) to the progression of the rally.

And speaking of tennis...

Why was an improvisational actor working with professional athletes?

Hold on. We're almost there.

Performing at the *Improv Asylum* gave me the opportunity to teach in the training center as well as the chance to learn the application of these principles as a corporate training tool.

It resonated. Big time!

After my first few classes as a student in the training center I remember going into work and thinking differently. It seemed so clear and obvious to me that the principles that are so effective on stage are no different than at work. Better yet, what would a work environment look like that was built on "yes, and?" As much as I enjoyed myself on stage, these principles were so much bigger than entertainment. So, in addition to performing and getting to entertain audiences using these principles, I took advantage of every class I could teach and volunteered for every possible corporate training session.

I left the *Improv Asylum* and moved to Florida in 2003, and it didn't take long before I befriended two other talented performers and we began our own improvisation group. One of my partners owned the theater where we performed, taught drama and improvisation to kids and adults, and offered corporate training workshops.

It was during this same time that an old college friend of mine approached me about serving as the emcee for an international conference she was hosting in

Washington, DC. She had started an organization called *WorldBlu* whose mission was to celebrate freedom-centered companies while helping to inspire and train people how to become freedom-centered leaders.

The *WorldBlu* mission sounded like a big "yes, and" to me so I jumped in with both feet. Saying "yes, and" to that opportunity opened a door to a corporate world that never seemed possible. These were global companies, hugely successful Fortune 500 and 100 companies who did things a different way - and were at the top of their industry.

Saying "yes, and" gave me the opportunity to see how these companies did things with a different model emphasizing culture, values, and engagement. Although the language was different, I could see each freedom-centered principle as another reinforcement of an improvisation "yes, and" mindset. This proved to be yet another valuable progression in my "yes, and" evolution.

My work with *WorldBlu* led me into a rigorous leadership training that really forced me to evaluate and articulate my purpose and mission. The extensive training served as a game changer for my life and career. After three years of leadership coaching and training I made the decision to become a life coach. I found great satisfaction in being able to help individuals overcome obstacles that were getting in the way of their true happiness and potential.

The more I grew as a life coach the more I began to see the natural integration of the improvisational principles in my coaching practice. When it came right down to it, the same ideas that worked on stage also helped someone get unstuck in their professional or private life.

This line of work led me to take an assistant coaching soccer position at my college alma mater, which turned into a mentoring role for high school students over the next three years.

In less than 10 years, from the time of my first improv class, I had taken this idea of "yes, and" and found powerful significance and application for its use on stage, in the workplace, in sports, in life, and in all relationships. I felt like I was on to something.

When I had the courage to step away from my high school mentoring position in 2012, my wife and I had no idea what was going to come next, but we knew it had to grow the idea of "yes, and." I had already started a series of online programs called *30 Days of YES* that were designed to help people articulate and live their purpose. But I really yearned for the opportunity to teach and speak and share my message in a broader way.

In early 2013 when a friend sent me a job posting with the title "Improvisation and Leadership Coach," I thought it was a joke. Seriously, have you ever heard of a job with leadership and improvisation in the same title? Better yet, we had just moved back to Florida, and this job was in Florida.

It was for a Leadership and Improvisation Coach at IMG Academy. I knew IMG Academy. I had attended a one week camp in high school. I knew the history, I knew the excellence, and I knew what kind of opportunity this was.

I applied for the job with no anxiety. In the past I may have felt stress or a real attachment to the outcome, but in all honesty, I wasn't looking for a job. I was content to keep working for myself and growing my practice, but this seemed like a unique opportunity.

Through the interview process I was able to stay honest and authentic. Since I wasn't attached to the outcome it freed me up to just be myself. I wasn't trying to impress them with my answers, so I just relaxed and enjoyed the experience.

Throughout the interviews I just kept thinking ..."If there is a more qualified person than me - I want to meet them!"

That sounds really arrogant, but I really felt in my heart this job was created for me. Up until that point in my professional life I looked at my career path as random at best, and probably irresponsible to most. Then, out of nowhere a job comes along with a job description from my diary.

During the interview process I was also very curious as to why they felt they needed an improvisation and leadership coach. What did they really want to achieve?

IMG Academy had the need to replace a company that had been providing leadership and improvisation training to their students. The company, *Game On*, had provided these services for years and established the value and effectiveness of teaching kids confidence, body language, interview skills, and teamwork through improvisation and theater games. Once that partnership ended, IMG Academy decided to create their own in-house Leadership Department to help shift the focus not just on personal presence skills, but to emphasize the leadership aspect as well. Those just happened to be the two areas that were my (no so random after all) sweet spots!

I got the job and moved the family from the east coast to the west coast of Florida. And for the next few years I got to work at one of the top performance facilities in the world, teaching and coaching students from all countries in many sports, professional athletes, and leaders from companies in all industries.

All the world's a stage…

I often tell people that the rush I felt on the soccer field is similar to the high I get while performing on stage. Two different arenas, but both performances. I would ask kids before class if they see themselves as actors, and very few if any would raise their hands. Then I'd ask them to stand up and walk around the room with confidence, and they immediately would snap into perfect confident body language as they strutted around the space.

We often mistake acting for that thing done on stage and screen, and we forget that we act our way through our day-to-day lives. Working with these athletes I got the opportunity to help them see themselves as performers in and out of their sport. Getting them up on their feet and out of their comfort zone helped build a greater sense of confidence and personal presence.

The athletes learned that authentic leaders inspire others with their ability to draw forth contribution and engagement from everyone on the team, making them feel valued and respected in the process. They learned what it means to make their teammate look brilliant.

And of course, these athletes learned the power of "yes, and." They got to experience firsthand the value of collaborating as a team, finding agreement, and building off each others ideas. In the process they discovered that in order to have "yes, and" with a teammate it requires trust, respect, confidence, courage, humility, compassion, and empathy (just to name a few). These are the qualities that help you excel on and off the field, and just happen to be the same qualities that make improvisation possible.

That is why one of the top sports facilities in the world hired an improviser - because performance is performance. Whether you are hitting a 90 mph fastball, running a company, playing in a concert, desiring to be a better parent, or standing up to give a speech...

All the world's a stage...

It is all performance. Your life is a role made just for you, and you are the star! For nearly a dozen years I couldn't see how all of the dots of my life would align to create anything that made sense. I was committed to my purpose and living it as authentically as possible, but it still didn't make sense.

I am serious when I say that first improv class changed my life. I thought I was signing up to pursue a passion that might turn into a fun hobby, but never imagined it would transform how I approach every aspect of my life. Through each professional and personal up and down I was saying "yes" to each situation that arose, and doing my best to respond with an "and" that was on purpose. I didn't realize that the struggle I often felt was the training that was needed to demonstrate living a "yes, and" life.

I never imagined that finding "yes, and" in the *Improv Asylum* theater would send me on a journey to where I am today life coaching and working with professional athletes, corporate leaders, and people with diverse backgrounds from all over the world. And what these years have taught me is that the principles of "yes, and" apply to anyone and everyone, because at the end of the day…

*All the world's a stage…*and your life is the performance!

So, let's shift the focus to you!

UN*STUCK* Principle #2:

Life is the Performance!

Chapter 3:

There Are No Mistakes

Say yes and you'll figure it out afterwards. —Tina Fey

Now that we understand the basis of "yes, and" and how it applies to improvisation, it is time to go deeper and discover how this relates to your day to day life.

If you remember from the last chapter...

YES = Acceptance of the offer.

AND = Adding new information to the offer.

There is your "yes, and" right there. Simple. Straightforward.

As an improviser you work from the mantra that there are no mistakes. They are impossible. Since everything happening is new and there is no script, there can be no mistakes. Great improvisers understand this and realize that brilliant scenes often come from so-called mistakes that are justified and turned into genius.

Learning this idea for the first time was so refreshing. Imagine, there are no mistakes. *So, whatever is happening right now is perfect and is exactly what is supposed to be happening - right now.*

Take that in for a moment.

And as you pause I can hear all of the objections you have to that statement. It is that word "perfect" which might be hard to swallow. When we hear the word "perfect" we associate it with "good" and "pleasurable." If something is perfect there is a good chance we are enjoying it. But, if I am dealing with a real difficult situation right now, or if someone is in actual physical pain, how is that perfect?

"That is great for the stage Travis, but how does it really apply to real life situations? Can my struggles really be perfect?"

YES...

And...

It might just change how you respond to every situation from here on out.

A few years back while in the middle of my unemployment, I was eating lunch at a little Mexican cantina in Florida. This was an extremely difficult time for me. I was stuck with no real sense of direction. Yearning for inspiration, I was reading

Eckhart Tolle's *A New Earth* when this passage struck a powerful chord in me:

Life will give you whatever experience is most helpful for the evolution of your consciousness. How do you know this is the experience you need? Because this is the experience you are having at the moment.

I probably looked a little crazy because I began to chuckle out loud as tears filled my eyes. The words spoke directly to what I was feeling and struggling with.

Being unemployed is one thing, but not having a plan is another. I felt like a failure, and spent most of my time beating myself up and second guessing all of the choices I was making.

Reading that quote felt like a wave of freedom washing over me. In my heart I always listened and prayed to be led to where I needed to be, and reading that passage reminded me that I was indeed exactly in my rightful place. Up until that point I had associated my personal struggle with failure, instead of seeing it as a growth opportunity. More than just being optimistic or having faith, it reinforced the improv principle that there are no mistakes. Even if my current circumstances weren't what I envisioned, I still had the ability to collaborate with my situation instead of denying it.

Mistakes are only mistakes when we label them as such. Or, we can embrace the reality that mistakes are often the gateway for innovation and invention, and keep moving in that direction.

Tomorrow might be different, but wherever you are tomorrow, that is where you are supposed to be as well. That's not a mistake either!

Now, let's connect this to an event in your own life.

Take a moment and think of the most difficult situation or event you have ever experienced.

Do you have it?

Now, I am not going to discount or trivialize any life event or tragedy you may have experienced.

Stay with me.

Whatever situation you are thinking of in your head, odds are it doesn't feel good. In fact, just thinking of it now may conjure up some difficult feelings and memories.

Let me ask you this…

Have you moved past this situation? Even if it still hurts, have you been able to move past it and get on with your life, or is it still holding you back?

If you feel you have been able to move forward it means you accepted, at some point, that whatever you were dealing with indeed was real and was happening.

Meaning, you weren't in denial. This is huge. All of us know what it means to experience denial. If you have uttered any of these phrases, you have been in denial:

This can't be happening!

Why is this happening to me?

This shouldn't be happening!

There must be a mistake.

These are all classic denial statements. If you are human, you have felt or voiced one if not all of these statements at one time or another. It doesn't make you a bad person, it just means you were stuck in a moment of denial.

When I think of denial I can't help but think of this exchange in one of my favorite comedic movies, *National Lampoon's Christmas Vacation.* Chevy Chase's character Clark is talking with his wife Ellen about their eccentric brother-in-law Eddie and his inability to have Christmas gifts for his own kids.

Clark: *"How can they have nothing for their children?"*

Ellen: *"Well, he's been out of work for close to seven years."*

Clark: *"In seven years, he couldn't find a job?"*

Ellen: *"Catherine says he's been holding out for a management position."*

That is denial.

So, back to you. Have you been able to move on from your situation, or are you still stuck like Cousin Eddie?

The truth is, we are unable to make any progress until we accept reality.

In improvisation, saying "yes" means accepting your partner's offer.

In life, saying "yes" means accepting reality.

Now, let me give you a lot of clarification around that statement.

I grew up with a spiritual faith background that vehemently denied "accepting a reality" based on the physical picture. If the physical picture did not match spiritual truth, than it must not be real. Honestly, this worked very well for me, but I also saw how taking this idea out of context caused lots of problems for many.

So, when I talk about reality, I simply mean "what appears to be happening."

No judgment. No value. Just the facts.

If you have been laid-off, the reality is "you have lost your job." If you have been diagnosed with cancer, the reality is you "have cancer." If your wife is filing for a divorce, the reality is "you are getting a divorce." If you have just won the Powerball. The reality is "you are now a millionaire."

That is what is happening. Good or bad, those are the facts before us.

I can make it even simpler than that.

Where are you right now?

I am sitting in a recognizable coffee shop featuring a mermaid in their logo. This is where I am as I write this. Therefore, this is the reality that is going on right now.

I accept these facts as my current situation, therefore I am in total agreement with reality right now.

YES = Accepting reality

Just as in improvisation, I don't need to like what is happening, but I must accept it.

The acceptance is huge. By accepting what is happening it now gives me the ability to respond to it. When we are in denial, we are unable to consider solutions because we cannot address something that we don't admit is real.

Or, to put it in a statement that rhymes...

You cannot progress until you say YES!

As long as we turn away from reality and sit in denial it is impossible to address the need at hand.

Remember this from Peter Block, *"The answer to how is yes!"* Now, go back to the difficult situation you thought of in your head. If you were able to move forward, at some point you had to say "yes - this is happening."

I challenge you to think of a situation where you were able to make any progress while still being in denial of the facts.

Yeah, me neither.

For four years of college soccer I was in denial of my situation. I loved soccer, and to this day count it as one of my favorite passions. Yet, for four years I fooled myself into believing that my coach was the cause of my problems, not me.

Each year I would report to soccer camp ready for a new season. I would start off playing with confidence and joy, and end the season mentally frazzled and miserable.

My coach had an idea of what it meant to be a successful player on his team. That meant being physically tough and fearless on the field. I had always seen myself as a technically skilled player who understood the game. That may have been true, but the demand on me was to add the physical element to my game in order to compete at that level.

The problem was, I was in denial. I loved soccer, but playing the way he wanted me to play seemed too difficult and intimidating. In my heart I wanted to figure it out, but I really didn't know how. So, instead of really digging in and admitting I needed help, I chose denial.

I hoped that my other skills would balance out the physical play, but they didn't. I was mad, frustrated, discouraged, and not short on blame for how my coach needed to change to meet my style.

How do you think that worked out for me?

So, instead of playing and excelling at the game I loved, I floundered. Although I never quit, I was tempted on numerous occasions. My inability to accept the facts had me considering every possible option besides the obvious one…

Saying "yes" to reality.

Saying yes in this situation would have been accepting that I needed to be a more physical player.

Again, I didn't need to like it, but I needed to accept it. Accepting it meant getting outside of my comfort zone and admitting that I needed to evolve. It also meant getting past my own ego that had created an impressive argument of why everyone else was in the wrong except me.

And, since you cannot progress until you say yes, guess who didn't progress?

For nearly 15 years after my playing days were over I would occasionally have a reoccurring dream that I was given one more year of eligibility to go back and redeem myself. Then I would wake up and realize it was a dream…or nightmare.

There was no going back. That ship had sailed long ago. As a coach both at the high school and college level I saw plenty of guys who struggled with the same issue I experienced. And as a coach, I understood where my coach was coming from during those four years. He was right. If I had been in his shoes, I would have treated me the same way (Don't worry, it only took me over 10 years of my life to figure that one out).

Remember, saying "yes" doesn't mean you have to like the facts, but it allows you to face them. And by facing them we can now choose how we need to respond.

And that leads us to the "and!"

YES = Accepting reality

In improvisation, the "and" was adding new information to the offer.

In life, saying "and" means you choose your response!

AND = Choosing your response!

Yes, you actually have a choice!

Go back to the difficult situation you've been thinking about this chapter. If you were in denial, you were unable to choose any response. You were denying its existence. But, if you did accept it as happening, how did you choose to respond to it?

This is where you have power.

People believe that we control certain aspects of our life, but we don't. We don't control anything that happens to us, but we have *infinite possibilities* when it comes to our response.

It's your choice (only and ever 100% of the time).

There are no mistakes. Think about those difficult situations and now view them through the lens of "there are no mistakes." Ask yourself, what did I learn as a result of going through that experience? How am I a better or stronger person from the lessons I learned?

What may have felt like a mistake at the time gave you exactly what you needed to respond to where you are now. So, was it really a mistake then?

I was working with a football player a few years back before the NFL Combine. He shared how he dealt with adversity during tough games. He went on to share that during high school his mother dealt with cancer. He was forced to become the man of the house and would spend many nights at his mom's side caring for her needs.

As a high profile college athlete he would think of her often during tough moments in games. Whenever he got too down, he would remember how his mom battled through the disease and eventually beat it, and it allowed him to put the weight of the moment in perspective. Thinking of his mom allowed him to calm his nerves, settle down, and perform.

During those tough years he had to accept that "yes" indeed his mom was battling cancer. And in response to the situation he used it as fuel and motivation for overcoming his own adversity. By saying "yes, and" he was able to work his way through one of the worst situations imaginable and turn it into inspiration in order to live out his childhood dream of playing football on Sundays. Mom is still cheering him on.

He had no choice with the cancer, but numerous options when it came to his response.

In fact, here are just a few ways he could have chosen to respond:

* Giving up on his life dream
* Quitting football all together
* Falling into negativity and blaming others
* Playing the role of a victim for the rest of his life

Why me?

Can you remember a time when you played the role of the victim? (You can't see me, but I am also raising my hand.)

We all have. It makes us human.

Playing the role of a victim doesn't make you a bad person, it just means you are stuck. It means that you have been fooled into thinking you don't have a choice in how to respond, but you do.

As a soccer player I knew in my heart I had a choice, but making that choice seemed too difficult. It was a lot easier to play the role of the victim. Instead of taking control of my response, I opted for denial and believing that I didn't have a choice.

It's not my fault, it's the coach!

By making my coach the scapegoat in my mind it gave me an excuse for not needing to change anything in myself. It is much easier to blame someone else for our shortcomings than it is to actually take responsibility for them and make some difficult but necessary changes.

Had I only said "yes, and" to my college soccer coach, it may have looked like this...

Yes, I need to become a more physical player.

And, please help me with how I can overcome some of my doubts and fears.

By being in acceptance with reality I could have chosen a response that addressed the problem.

You cannot progress until you say yes!

Or, as Tina Fey is quoted at the top of this chapter...

Say yes and you'll figure it out afterwards.

She doesn't say "how" you'll figure it out, and we already know that "yes" is the answer to "how."

I no longer have reoccurring dreams of getting another year of college eligibility. I have made peace with the choices (or lack thereof) I made during those four years, and have chosen to "and" them by not making the same mistake in other areas of my life.

Coach Johnson, I hope you are reading this. It took me awhile, but I finally figured it out.

If this sounds too easy, you're almost right.

It is simple, but not easy.

When you are stuck in the middle of a difficult situation, it is easy to get trapped and feel like a victim. Instead of arguing with reality and seeing it as a mistake we have the opportunity to embrace the challenge and see it as an opportunity for growth and discovery.

Moving forward, let's look more closely at these dark moments of our life and see what is really going on, and how bringing a "yes, and" mindset just might open a world of possibility.

UN*STUCK* Principle #3:

> *There Are No Mistakes!*
> *(You cannot progress until you say "Yes!")*

Chapter 4:

Embrace the Goo!

*Just when the caterpillar thought the world was over,
it became a butterfly.* —*English Proverb*

A few years back I fell in love with the metaphor of
the butterfly. It's not that I hadn't thought of it before,
but I had never taken the time to investigate what
was really happening during that caterpillar to
butterfly transformation.

To be honest, I figured that the caterpillar created the
cocoon, and then while in the cocoon it morphed into
a butterfly, cracked out of the cocoon, and flew on its
way.

Not quite.

Clearly I am not an entomologist (and thank you
spellcheck for helping me get that correct).

Bear with me though, we have a lot to learn from the
metamorphosis of the caterpillar.

Life begins.

The caterpillar's job is to eat and eat and eat. It
consumes all it can handle in order to go through a

series of molts where it grows new and bigger skin underneath its old skin. The old skin falls away and is immediately replaced by the new.

This happens a number of times before the caterpillar creates its own cocoon.

Now, let's take a time out from science here for a moment.

I want you to play the role of the caterpillar. You are born, going through life, and doing what you are supposed to do. You eat, get bigger, explore your environment, and life seems pretty simple.

Then one day, something is not right. You can feel growth taking place, but it's different. You expect to see a new coat of skin, but instead you find yourself imprisoned within your own tomb. This can't be good.

Change is taking place and you have no say in the matter. How do you feel? Are you scared? Do you feel uncertain? Do you welcome the change?

There is a real possibility that you even feel this is the end. Besides, that cocoon looks an awful lot like a coffin.

Okay, back to the science.

The caterpillar creates its own chrysalis, and this is where things get juicy, or should I say…

Gooey!

While in the chrysalis state the body of the caterpillar begins to liquify. It turns into a black goo. Now get this, scientists claim that the goo is rich with nutrients and potential.

Potential!

In fact, the cells of the caterpillar responsible for this change are called imaginal cells. The imaginal cells are different than the cells present for the previous molts. These cells carry different information than the previous cells and even vibrate at a different frequency. I am not making this up.

At first the caterpillar's immune system perceives the imaginal cells as enemies and begins to attack them, but to no avail. Inside the chrysalis the imaginal cells take over and fully transform the caterpillar.

Okay, another science time-out!

Remember, you are the caterpillar. Your body has already created its own coffin, and you feel the changes taking place must be a virus or sickness of some kind. Now, to add to the picture, most of your body has dissolved into a black goo.

How are you feeling about life right now? Feeling a little bleak?

Is any part of you welcoming this change?

Even the most positive of caterpillars must be thinking, "This ain't good! It was fun while it lasted."

In your best Jim Morrison you mutter to yourself...

This is the end, my only friend, the end...

Back to science!

The imaginal cells complete the metamorphosis. The black goo which was rich in nutrients and potential have transformed the caterpillar into a brand new life form - the butterfly.[1]

Newly transformed, the butterfly hatches from his cocoon that can no longer hold him, pauses for awhile to let its wings dry, and then turns upright and flies away to a new life and experience.

This is not a caterpillar with wings and an antennae. It is a completely new form. Totally changed and evolved. Transformed.

---

[1] http://imaginal-labs.com/imaginal-cells/

What appeared on the surface to be death and darkness was actually the necessary process for transformation. There was no shortcut. In order for the caterpillar to fulfill its destiny of becoming a butterfly it needed to experience the goo.

It had no choice.

Okay, science lesson over. Back to you.

I have no idea what that experience must feel like for the caterpillar, but I don't imagine it as a subtle process.

The goo is messy. The goo is scary. The goo is necessary.

And the goo is good!

I invite you to think of the goo experiences in your life. Perhaps it was an event that happened years ago, or it may even be an event happening right now.

What does your goo look like?

When I think of my own goo experiences I can't help but think of my almost 4 years without having a full-time job and regular income. This is the situation I referred to in the last chapter.

In 2003 my wife and I moved from Boston to Florida with our newborn daughter. I was working for a Web site at the time and was grateful that I was able to carry my work with me. Within six months of being in Florida we found our dream home, moved in, and discovered my wife was pregnant with our second child. 9 months later we welcomed child number two to the family, and then a few months after that I was let go from my job.

Not quite the way I planned it.

Truth be told, I had been contemplating leaving my job for awhile, but I didn't know what the next career chapter looked like. Ideally it would have been nice to have a new opportunity waiting in the wings, and then time the transition seamlessly.

Somehow, life didn't get the memo.

I embraced the change, but I didn't have a plan. I was inspired to pursue new opportunities, but I didn't know what those looked like.

It was during those few weeks of contemplation that I was approached by Traci at *WorldBlu* to host her 2005 conference. Saying "yes" to that opportunity put the wheels in motion that eventually led to my leadership training and eventual life coaching practice.

But hold on. That process took a few years.

During this time, although inspired by everything I was learning and experiencing, we struggled!

Over the span of the next four years I worked hard at generating opportunities, but not much materialized. Work would come, but never enough. Things looked promising, but rarely panned out.

My wife and I watched as our savings that had been so carefully acquired quickly disappeared. Not only did it disappear, it turned into debt. And just for fun measure, we had another child (for which I am extremely grateful).

Now, I don't like embellishing stories, but just when things couldn't get worse, the financial collapse of 2007 happened. Yup, there weren't a lot of people looking to spend extra money on life coaches during that time. So, despite following my heart and passion, looking for whatever work I could manage, and chasing every lead, I ran out of ideas and options. This led us to the toughest decision we never wanted to make. We had to leave our home.

Without any leads coming to fruition, I took a seasonal job serving as the assistant soccer coach at my alma mater in St. Louis. It was only a four month position, but I was desperate. Plus, I loved being a coach.

Because of the real estate situation we were nearly upside down on our house payment. The rental market was healthy so we were able to keep our house rented while we found a cheap rental in St. Louis. I still get a pit in my stomach when I think of having to box up and leave our dream home.

One night before leaving for St. Louis my wife broke down in bed from the sadness of having to move. It broke my heart. I had no plan, no real way of comforting her and making her feel better. In total honesty and vulnerability all I could tell her is that no matter where we live, as long as the five of us are together, it's all the home we needed.

It was a painful goo moment.

I had so many questions that I didn't have the answers to. I carried the burden of feeling irresponsible and not being able to adequately provide for my family. I felt like a failure.

Yet, even in the gooiest of the goo, I was conscious of the experience. I remember having a number of conversations with people during this time and sharing how I was processing the situation. Although I just wanted the financial suffering to end, I was aware that the moment was rich with potential.

What was I learning?

That is a question I asked myself over and over again. Despite the pain I felt watching my life savings disappear and fall into debt, I was still a happy and joyful person. I felt gratitude and appreciation, even in the midst of all the fear and uncertainty. It wasn't easy, but even with all of the darkness I could still see and feel the light.

This felt like a key learning moment.

I felt my identity and concept of career, life, and family being challenged in a big way. I had gone through many transitions in my adult life, but this felt different. In this scenario I really didn't have any answers. I couldn't connect the dots. Things looked bleak, and there didn't seem to be light at the end of the tunnel. Heck, where in the hell was the tunnel?

Looking back I imagine it felt a lot like what the caterpillar feels like entering his cocoon - dark, cramped, and scary.

Loading up the moving truck and standing in our empty house was a sad day. Neighbors hugged us as we left, and my poor wife could barely keep it together as we pulled away from the house.

If I were turning this into a "happily ever after" story I would explain that the move to St. Louis proved to be a glorious turning point.

It wasn't.

In fact, after my four-month season ended I took another high school part-time coaching position that paid less than the previous job. And it wasn't enough to pay the bills. One month we relied on the grace and kindness of friends to help us pay our rent.

It was incredibly humbling.

There are plenty of memories in my head during that period where I felt completely lost, having no idea of what the next step would look like. My faith was continually being put to the test. And once the high school coaching position ended there was nothing waiting for me.

Nothing.

I applied for a few positions, but nothing landed.

We ended up moving in with our in-laws for a few months while I continued to look for work. The position that finally opened up was for a boarding school houseparent.

You cannot progress until you say yes!

So, of course I said yes!

For the next three years my family of five lived in an apartment of a boys dormitory where I parented and mentored high school boys from around the world. It was demanding work with very low pay. So, it was a win-win.

Although it was the furthest thing from being financially lucrative, it helped stop the bleeding. It gave us an opportunity to exhale a little bit and ground ourselves in one spot for a few years. I was not sure how long the chrysalis phase was going to last, but I knew I was still in the goo. Humbly, I kept asking myself the question...

What am I learning?

The truth is, I was learning a whole heck of a lot.

For starters, as bleak as the situation had been for those number of years, the family was fine. The kids were happy. Our marriage was strong. In fact, I am blessed to say that those years of turmoil only brought my wife and I closer together.

During those years we saw a number of other marriages fail under similar circumstances and pressure, so I felt gratitude to have such a strong partner in my corner. Despite my guilt of feeling like I wasn't providing for the family, Hollister always had my back. That was huge.

I was also learning the rich lesson of not being attached to titles, bank accounts, and status. I had no choice because I would have been 0 for 3.

My external identity was being stripped away to reveal my true authenticity. Who am I without a successful career, nice house, and fun toys?

My ego was taking a beating!

The truth is, I figured out I was still a pretty cool and interesting guy without all of the other material attachments. What a lesson this was for me to learn!

My true identity was being revealed. It was *who* I was "being," not *what* I was "doing." How was I showing up in my relationships and daily interactions? Was I still living with passion and purpose? Yes! That is the other huge piece I took away from this experience - I remained on purpose. This is a key connection because this is where "yes, and" and the goo come together.

During this time, as scary, painful, and humbling as it was, I never sacrificed or compromised my purpose and passion.

In fact, it forced me to say "yes, and" to situation after situation that I never would have chosen on my own.

Here is what some of those offers looked like that I had to say "yes, and" to:

Life: *You cannot afford to live in your home anymore.*

Travis: *Yes, and I will move the family to St. Louis.*

Life: *Your coaching position is only 4 months.*

Travis: *Yes, and I will learn as much as I can in that time!*

Life: *You have no job prospects. You are unemployed.*

Travis: *Yes, and we will move in to my in-laws place for a few months.*

Life: *Your new job pays peanuts.*

Travis: *Yes, and I will use this opportunity to hone my coaching skills.*

Yes, and…yes, and…yes, and!

This is where I think we often stumble and fall down. We confuse not liking what life is giving us with not having a choice.

That is a great lie.

We always have a choice. We don't have to "like" what life is giving us, but our "and" response is our choice. Our attitude is a choice.

I am curious about the caterpillars who enter their chrysalis but die in the transformation process. What is it that separates the caterpillars that die with those who transform?

My guess is that it depends on what happens in the goo. Since the goo is rich with nutrients and potential, the caterpillar still has a responsibility to act on that potential. If it is too attached to its old concept of life and form, perhaps it prevents the metamorphosis from taking place.

The goo is an offer that needs to be accepted with a glorious "yes!"

"And," I am going to grow some beautiful wings and break out of this shell!

Are you still with me?

Can you take a moment and think about some of the goo moments you are dealing with right now, and are you able to see the rich potential for growth that is calling you forth?

Saying "yes, and" to the goo is simple, but not easy.

As an improviser, you never know what is coming next. You can anticipate and influence, but there are infinite ideas and responses that can come your way. Some of them are brilliant, and some of them are gooey. Either way, the only way to move forward is by saying "yes, and."

People often ask me if I have ever bombed on stage? Hello! Yes, Yes, Yes! You are not a seasoned performer if you have not stunk up the stage many times. In fact, you are not a very good performer if you have never felt completely naked on stage and questioning your very existence after a performance. This is what builds your tough skin. These goo experiences are what allow you to go into intimidating environments and tell yourself, "I have dealt with things tougher than this - so bring it on!" And if you bomb again, it prepares you even more as your move forward learning and growing.

That is why the goo in our life is rich with nutrients and potential. Nutrients like what you find in manure, that literally turns shit into life! And potential, because these events on their own are indifferent, but when we choose to learn from them they propel us to another level. Nutrients and potential!

Now that we see that the goo is actually good, in the next chapter we'll explore how we can have more control of our "and" response.

UN*STUCK* Principle # 4:

Embrace the Goo!

Chapter 5:

Belief it!

Whether you think you can, or you think you can't--you're right. —Henry Ford

The goo is adversity. That word, "adversity" has become such a cliche catch- phrase in the world of sports used by almost any athlete doing an interview.

In fact, let me go ahead and write a post-game interview response and notice if it sounds familiar…

You know, we've had to deal with a lot of adversity this year. We had a bulls-eye on our back all season, and no one was giving us a chance. So many times our backs were against the wall, but that's when we are at our best. We just kept believing in ourselves and working hard, and here we are. We shocked the world!

Sound familiar?

Elite athletes understand the real value of adversity. Adversity makes you stronger. Without adversity, without distractions, without the resistance and push-back from an opponent, it is difficult to maintain the motivation needed to sustain success. And, it's impossible to get better without it.

Your life is no different.

The goo is adversity. And, as difficult as it is to accept in those dark times, we know that the goo makes us stronger.

You are the person you are today in part because of the difficult circumstances you have endured, and the lessons that have come as a result.

Let's go back to the middle of my unemployment. Although brutal, I was conscious the whole time of the gift this difficulty was presenting to me. Granted, most of the time I wished I could return the gift, but I knew in my heart that this difficult experience was going to be a transformative learning opportunity. And it was. It stretched me far outside of my comfort zone and forced me to evolve whether I liked it or not.

I can honestly say I wouldn't be writing this book today if it weren't for those difficult years. And, it's not like they are done. Adversity doesn't stop. Even while writing and revising this book I have dealt with a few kicks in the gut, and I know I have a lifetime more to endure. So, it's not a matter of eliminating adversity, but adapting our attitude of how we respond.

Resistance is futile.

Things are going to be tough, that is inevitable.

Will you say "yes" to them as they come, and more importantly, what will your "and" look like?

Let's have some fun and play with that!

Here is a frightening scenario. Stay with me. Let's say I raised you and a friend in a house with no windows and no internet (okay, which is scarier, the no windows or no internet?) I am not an evil person. This just happens to be our living conditions for this example.

Today is the big day. I tell you that you get to go outside for 10 minutes and write down everything that you see. We have talked about all of the wonderful things in the outside world, but you have never seen them. Trees, people, flowers, animals, the sun, clouds, etc.

Before you go outside I remind you of that powerful thing called the "sun" and I give you these things called "glasses" to protect your eyes. You are so excited to explore that you grab them, run outside, and begin writing down everything that you see. You didn't notice that the lenses were pink. But the lenses I gave your friend are blue.

After 10 minutes the two of you come back inside. You are so excited to share how you saw trees, flowers, animals, and everything else on your adventure. I begin to ask you about what you saw, and every time I ask you the color of the object, what do you say?

Pink!

That's right! The people. Pink! Animals. Pink. Trees, flowers, dirt. Pink, pink, pink!

Your friend begins to argue with you and tries to convince you that you are wrong. None of those things were pink. They were blue! You go round and round for minutes, but you never give in. You know in your heart of hearts what you saw, and everything was pink!

Okay, end of scary scenario.

But, who is right? You or your friend?

Intellectually, we all know that you both are right, and yet wrong at the same time. It all depended on your lens. At the end of the day, your lens is your lens, and mine is mine. Who is right is simply subjective.

The problem is we too often mistake our strong opinions for fact or truth. We hold our opinions with such conviction that we don't allow ourselves to entertain another perspective.

Let's take this a step deeper. Where does our perspective come from? How did we form these opinions?

Life events. Religion. School. Culture. Previous history. Parents. Upbringing. Research. All true.

But I want to go a little deeper than that.

It is our beliefs.

Our beliefs are mainly responsible for what creates our opinions and perspective.

Important to note, our beliefs aren't necessarily true. All you need to do is have a political discussion to realize that beliefs and truth are not the same thing.

Remember, for thousand of years it was believed that the world was flat. It was believed and then taught. And, when we believe something - it then impacts our behavior and action. It becomes our truth, even if it's not necessarily true.

Sailors were instructed to not sail too far into the distance for fear of falling off the face of the earth. The fact that we all know the expression, "They fell off the face of the earth," is proof that this was an idea widely believed.

Belief created perception. Perception impacted behavior and action. (But our perception doesn't change truth.)

The same is going on in your life right now based on your own beliefs. I could write an entire book on beliefs vs. truth, but it's already been done (see Plato and Socrates).

Let's keep moving forward.

So, there is YOU! Then there are your BELIEFS.

Let's continue on with the idea that your beliefs are equivalent to the color of your lens. Whether you want to see those as glass lenses or contact lenses, it is up to you. Same impact. The way you see the world is through your beliefs.

On the other side of your beliefs is life.

In this case, life is simply the facts of what is happening. There is no value or judgment to the facts. They are just the facts.

For instance, the reality of life right now is that I am sitting in a coffee shop, it is 2:44 pm, I am wearing clothes, there are other people here, it is rainy outside, and my coffee cup is empty.

Those are some of the facts of this moment.

None of them are either good or bad, they just are what they are. No value, no judgement.

Yet, when I view all of these facts through the lens of my perspective (beliefs) I begin to give each of them different value.

I am sitting in a coffee shop = I love this coffee shop!

It's is 2:44pm = Shoot! This is bad, I am going to be late.

I am wearing clothes = These jeans are getting a little worn.

There are other people here = I love my baristas, but the woman next to me is too loud.

It's rainy outside = I like the rain, we needed it badly!

My coffee cup is empty = That was delicious. Time for a refill.

The point is, the facts are just the facts until WE add value to them. Period.

My coffee cup being empty is neither good or bad until I decide it one way or another. Even indifference is an opinion, just not a very passionate one.

I think we all understand this idea at a basic level, but we quickly forget it. You and I are sitting on the beach when a dog runs up. If you like dogs, you will probably be excited. If I dislike dogs, I will probably be annoyed.

Same beach. Same dog. Two different opinions.

It is not the dog or beach itself that is either good or bad, but rather our opinion that we project on them.

Here is what happens next. You experience life, and based on your perspective, you project your opinion. As a result of our beliefs, we tend to respond in one of two ways.

The following thought patterns reflect two tracks of thought. See if you can relate to either one.

The Victim Mindset

The victim mindset is exactly as it sounds. The characteristics, attitudes, and responses include:

- Negativity
- Anger/Frustration
- Discouragement
- Apathy
- Blame
- Complaint
- Make excuses

The mantra of the victim is: *There is nothing I can do!*

The big 3! If you want to know quickly whether or not you are in a victim mindset - just look for **Blaming, Complaining, and Making Excuses!**

Those three are a tell-tale sign you are stuck and behaving like a victim. In this response you are lashing out to everything and everyone around you, even yourself. You need to pass the blame in order to protect your ego.

The sun was in my eyes!

It's the economy's fault!

Coach should have played me more.

My parents didn't push me hard enough.

My professor had it out for me.

I knew I wasn't any good. I should have never tried!

This weather is making me grumpy.

When you respond to a situation from this victim mindset it is nearly impossible to find a successful solution. The blaming, complaining, and making excuses is a clever tool the ego uses to prepare itself for failure. It is already in damage control and thinking of ways to deflect the pain that comes with taking ownership.

Does this sound like anyone you know?

Does this ever sound like you?

Of course it does, and it doesn't make you a bad person, it just means you are stuck.

When you are stuck in the victim mindset too long, you may eventually find yourself quitting.

(Do you know how many times I sat down to write a book before sticking this one out?)

I have worked with hundreds of kids and adults in sessions where I have challenged them to an activity of skill, like singing. I then told them they would need to perform it in front of their peers to find out who is the best. The entire activity was set up to create pressure and competition and see how they responded to the challenge. Even though there was nothing really at stake, besides their pride, there were numerous times when people refused to take the challenge. They were so concerned about failing and looking silly that they quit and did not participate.

Even as you read this, the thought of having to stand up and sing in front of others may sound terrifying. It is supposed to. In fact, when I do this as an activity I don't actually make anyone sing, I just make them think they will have to. Every once in awhile I come across a brave soul who isn't afraid and they insist on singing even after I let them off the hook. These aren't necessarily musically-gifted people. They are not good singers; but for this particular activity they have chosen to show up with a different mindset.

That mindset is, of course, the Victor Mindset.

The Victor Mindset

If you thumb back and look at the characteristics of the victim mindset it is not difficult to figure out the qualities of the victor. The characteristics, attitudes, and responses include:

- Positivity
- Optimism
- Adaptable
- Flexible
- Energetic
- Accountable
- Taking Responsibility

The mantra of the victor is: *Do my best!*

The big 3 for the victor mindset is **Positivity, Adaptable, and Responsible!**

When you are operating in the victor mindset you are focused on learning and getting better. You are committed to doing your best and not getting distracted by the results. It is not that results don't matter, they do, but at the end of the day the victor uses every experience as an opportunity to improve.

Carol Dweck, the famous Stanford psychology professor has authored books on this response, calling it the "growth mindset." These are the same principles I worked from as a Leadership Specialist at IMG Academy to help athletes maximize their potential.

Our ego though doesn't want to think about learning opportunities. It wants validation about how cool and talented we are. If we are not, it needs a scapegoat to blame.

Working with so many athletes over the years it was easy to see which mindset was their stronger default response. I like to think of it this way. If we put our satisfaction on a scale of 1-10, all of us would have a default number where we land on a day to day basis. I think I am solidly planted between a 7 and 8. Now, depending on the events of the day it is only natural for my happiness to rise or drop a digit or two. And, of course, if something tragic or amazing occurs, the rise or spike will be much more drastic.

What I've found is that, no matter what happens, it is just a matter of time before we eventually return to our default setting. Human reason would suggest that the more good we experience, the higher we move on the happiness scale until we eventually break the scale.

If you were to ask someone what makes them happy, common answers include financial security, spending time with loved ones, and seeing the world.

By this rational, someone who was very wealthy, with lots of family, and traveled the world should consistently be showing up at a 10! Yet, I have encountered many people that meet all three criteria, but rank low on the satisfaction scale.

What gives?

Before we answer that and continue on, let's do another quick review.

We have…

You.

Your perspective (beliefs) of how you view the world.

Life. The events and facts of what is happening.

Response. Victor or victim?

Now we are caught up.

Again, what gives? If someone had family, financial security, and the ability to enjoy luxury, why are they not eternally happy?

When I introduce this session to younger students I always preface the presentation by calling this a "Billion Dollar Idea!" In fact, I encourage the students to steal this concept and make their billion dollars. I selflessly only want 1%.

When we break this concept down on the board I ask them where should we spend our time if we want to be happier...

On our beliefs...

or

on life events?

Without fail, the resounding answer is always on our beliefs!

Correct! Yahtzee! Eureka! Jackpot! Booyah!

If what is happening has no value, except the value we give it, then it is our beliefs that need continuous work, not what is happening. What is happening is valueless until our perspective gets involved.

Who is responsible for whether we respond as a victor or a victim?

Exactly. We are!

Our response is directly tied to our beliefs. Period. The reason so many people decline the singing challenge is because their thoughts run wild based on their beliefs. Thoughts like:

I cannot sing!

I am not talented!

I will make a fool of myself.

He is such a better singer than me.

It's not the singing, but our beliefs about us as singers. The negative and self-destructive thoughts are directly connected to limiting beliefs.

So, the people with limiting beliefs quickly move themselves down into the victim mindset.

Yes, getting stuck is a choice.

Conversely, those who believe they are capable and are committed to learning and doing their best will move themselves into the victor mindset.

It's simple, but not easy. That is why this is the billion dollar idea. All of us intellectually know that the key to success is in managing our beliefs and thoughts, yet time and again we focus our attention to whatever has happened to us most recently. Instead of handling our beliefs, we just end up judging what is.

As class is ending I warn my students to take a mental picture of this now, because it won't take much more than 30 seconds to fall back into the trap of blaming life events for our happiness.

Can you think of the last time this happened to you?

Today perhaps?

I have a friend who lost two of her children tragically in two separate car accidents. She has lived through the nightmare most parents fear, twice.

You would assume she would be a bitter and defeated woman; she is not. She is the exact opposite. She is light, a pure picture of joy and love. She is not in denial of what has happened, but she clearly understands that she gets to choose how she responds to life. As painful as it was to accept the events, she allowed herself to say "yes." She had no control over the events, but her "and" response is where she has claimed her power.

Victor or victim is a choice, a choice each of us makes dozens of times a day, everyday.

To understand this on an intellectual level is one thing - but to practice it is another. And, if you live anywhere in the western world, the culture sure doesn't help.

Turn on the television and you are bombarded with messages convincing you that the key to the happy life is improving who you are and what you have. We are all too familiar with the lure of trying to keep up with "The Jones'." Yet, I am pretty sure the Jones' aren't too happy either. Imagine that pressure of always trying to stay one step ahead of everyone who wants to be like you.

Most of us have felt that urge.

Commercial after commercial convincing us that we need a cooler car, newer iPhone, sexier spouse, exotic vacation, or new drug that will take away our pain.

I have yet to see a commercial that reinforces this message, "You are fine just the way you are, you just need to spend more time challenging your limiting beliefs about yourself."

It all comes back to your beliefs.

Nothing is either good or bad, but thinking makes it so. —
Shakespeare

Not sure if you've ever heard of this Shakespeare
fella, but he has some pretty good ideas. Remember
our dog on the beach. Good or bad? It doesn't really
matter except for what you believe.

Now, we could go around and try to change
everything we don't like. Good luck with that. If
anyone has ever had a spouse, child, boss, friend,
parent, teacher, co-worker...or any other relationship
involving another living thing - we all know how
successful it is to try to change them.

We have all gotten mad at the weather as well. *Yup,
how dare it rain on my wedding day!*

Or maybe traffic is your achilles. *Do all of these people
not realize I am in a hurry here?*

Whatever it is that creates a negative reaction in you
is simply tied back to your belief about it.

(Don't worry, this only applies to everything!)

Byron Katie, the creator of *The Work* and the author of
numerous books including *"Loving What Is"* describes
this concept of finding peace with what is happening.

Now, I could fill this book with quotes from Katie's books, but instead I'll just share two with you...

"A thought is harmless unless we believe it. It's not our thoughts, but our attachment to our thoughts, that causes suffering. Attaching to a thought means believing that it's true, without inquiring. A belief is a thought that we've been attaching to, often for years."

"As long as you think that the cause of your problem is "out there"—as long as you think that anyone or anything is responsible for your suffering—the situation is hopeless. It means that you are forever in the role of victim, that you're suffering in paradise."

Do me a favor, go back and reread those two quotes again.

Your beliefs are your perspective, and they are neither good or bad, until like Shakespeare adds, you give them your opinion - and make them so!

Life is just happening. Like your own custom made play, you are witnessing a world of events unfolding right before your eyes. It has no value until you color it with your perspective.

Instead of spending all of your time, energy, money, and life resisting it and trying to change it - say "Yes" to it and then choose the most powerful "and" response that brings you into alignment with your purpose and authenticity.

But how? How do we do this Travis?

By spending time exploring and examining your beliefs, and whether your beliefs are empowering you to a victor, or limiting you as a victim.

Which do you relate to most?

In the next chapter we'll look at some practical ways to take control of your thoughts and beliefs so that you can choose them, instead of letting them choose you!

UN*STUCK* Principle #5:

Belief it!

Chapter 6:

Good or bad, who knows?

Where Attention goes Energy flows; Where Intention goes Energy flows!
—James Redfield

It's time for an activity.

You need your watch or smartphone. Wherever you are sitting, I want you to spend the next 30 seconds counting the number of black objects around you.

Set your timer. Go.

(How are we doing?)

First of all, did you do it? Or, are you the person that sits there and skips ahead without doing the activity because you would rather just find out the point without actually participating? Shame on you.

If you did do the activity, how many black objects did you identify?

Odds are you did a pretty good job spotting a lot of black objects in your immediate space. If you happen to be locked up in a padded room and couldn't find any, I apologize, you are probably the exception.

Otherwise, you noticed some black objects. Now, to continue the activity, without taking any time to look around, tell me how many red objects are in the room.

Why the hesitation?

Go ahead and look around, notice all of the red. They pop out now, don't they?

So, when it came to knowing the number of black objects in the room you were probably more accurate and confident than noticing the red.

The reason is obvious. It was the black that you were focusing on for those 30 seconds. The red objects were there the whole time, you just weren't paying attention to them.

End of activity.

Where attention goes, energy flows!

This is a lesson I have shared with students and leaders hundreds of times over the years. It's not rocket science, just good old fashioned basic awareness.

The same applies in our day to day lives.

Let's replace "black objects" with "positive" experiences. And, let's replace "red objects" with "negative" experiences.

We have all been told since childhood that we need to focus on the good. If you are in a bad mood, focus on the good.

Again, this is simple stuff. It's common sense.

My good friend Justin Sua, the Head of Mental Conditioning for the Boston Red Sox often says...

It's common sense, but not common practice!

I love that! That has been my experience with coaching and leadership. We can all sit around and intellectualize common sense answers and solutions to our problems, but it is a little tougher putting them into practice.

On a typical day we are bombarded with endless events, interactions, and experiences. Yet, when we look back on our day we tend to only focus on a few key moments that determine our opinion. As a result we either label the day as "good" or "bad."

Let me ask you, what is it about a day that determines whether it was good or bad?

Think about our black and red objects again. They were both in the room at the same time, but you were only focusing on the black, so that is all you experienced. You cannot go throughout your day without any "bad" or negative things taking place, that is impossible. The billion dollar question is...

What are you choosing to focus on?

What are you giving you attention to on a moment to moment, day to day basis?

There is nothing either good or bad, but thinking makes it so.

Where Attention goes Energy flows; Where Intention goes Energy flows!

We cannot get rid of the "bad" or negative parts of our life, but we get to choose how we respond, and what we choose to focus on.

Let me give you one of my favorite stories. It has been retold in numerous ways, but it was told to me as a Chinese parable. It goes like this...

There is a farmer and his son. One day the son accidentally leaves the barn door open and all of the horses run away.

The neighbors hear of the event and come over to tell the farmer, "We heard about the horses. That is so bad!"

The farmer responds, "Good or bad, who knows?"

About a week later the horses return from the hills and have actually attracted some wild horses with them.

The neighbors come over and tell the farmer, "We heard about the new horses, that is so good!"

The farmer responds, "Good or bad, who knows?"

A week later the son tries to tame one of the wild horses, and in the process gets knocked off and breaks his shoulder.

The neighbors hear of the event and come over to tell the farmer, "We heard about your son. That is so bad!"

The farmer responds, "Good or bad, who knows?"

A year or so later the military comes to the farm to recruit young men to fight in the war, but due to his son's shoulder not healing properly he is unable to pass the physical.

The neighbors once again rush to the farmer and exclaim, "We heard about your son, that is so good!"

Once again, the farmer simply responds, "Good or bad, who knows?"

This is living "yes, and!" This is accepting was is happening instead of spending time resisting the facts.

Nothing is either good or bad, but thinking makes it so.

The events on their own are what they are, until we come along and color them with our lens.

The problem with this is that we constantly judge every experience from a very limited and small perspective. We don't allow ourselves to step back and ponder a bigger picture. The farmer in the story understands that each moment is connected to the next, which is connected to the next, and is infinitely connected to every other moment.

What appears "bad" and tragic one moment may actually serve as the gateway to an even better situation, which then opens another door to another experience and opportunity. It is never ending.

Can you remember a time when this has been true for you? What are some of your "good or bad, who knows" moments?

I look back on my life experiences and can remember so many events that I labeled "good" or "bad" like the neighbors in the story. Doing this opens us up to getting stuck with only viewing life from a limited perspective. We don't always get the luxury of looking back and connecting the dots. The lesson is to look at how we responded to each event when it happened. Did we "yes, and" or get stuck resisting the facts. What did we do with it? How did we choose to respond?

I have seen this happen in my life many times. Here are just two examples based on my career. I will break it down by telling you what *I thought was going to happen*, what *actually happened*, and then *how I responded* to the situation. Lastly, I'll share my big picture perspective of how I *reflect back* and connect the dots.

In 1997 my wife and I were in our first year of marriage living in Michigan. I was working for my dad's hamburger business, enjoying the opportunity to work side by side with my brother, but I knew in my heart that my wife and I didn't see Michigan as our home. My brother-in-law came along and offered me an opportunity to work at his sports facility in St. Louis.

What I thought was going to happen...

I thought I was going to love the job. My wife and I met in St. Louis so this felt like a great place to put our roots down for awhile. She found a job with a local city council woman and everything on paper looked great.

What actually happened…

It was brutal. I hated my job. My wife didn't like her job either. As a result my relationship with my sister and brother-in-law struggled.

How I responded…

Poorly at first. I withdrew contact from family because I regretted the decision to leave Michigan. Slowly though I took responsibility and was honest with my brother-in-law that I wasn't a good fit for the position. My wife and I expanded our job hunt and landed two jobs in Boston. After only 10 months in St. Louis, we were Boston-bound.

Reflecting back…

The move to St. Louis was not about the job, but rather my wife and I stepping out on our own and making a life for ourselves. Saying "yes" to the St. Louis opportunity opened the door for us to move forward, which led to finding jobs in Boston.

Once in Boston we embraced the excitement of city living and having new experiences. This was not a plan we had even considered 12 months previous. Professionally, Boston exposed me to the corporate world. And, most importantly, Boston is where I found my passion for improvisation. It is safe to say that I would not be sitting here preaching the value of "yes, and" if I had never said "yes" to St. Louis. Although messy and difficult at the time, the St. Louis step opened the door for the Boston opportunity to come along. Not exactly the way I would have mapped it out, but that is the point.

We don't use a map to navigate our life, only a compass.

Earlier in the book I shared my story of going from improv newbie, to eventually making it to the *Improv Asylum* Main Stage cast. What I left out of that story is how my time on the Main Stage came to an end.

It took me nearly three years to make it to the Main Stage cast, and less than a year for it to come to an end. My memories in that theater, on that stage, are some of the best of my life. Performing every weekend in front of sold-out audiences never got old, nor did getting paid for something I love to do. (I highly recommend it.)

But, before I got too settled in my new role it was announced that the cast would be cut in half. This meant more shows and more money if you made the cast, the only problem is I didn't make the cut. (Cue the carpet being pulled out from under my feet.)

This was tough news to handle. I won't say that I was devastated. It is show business and the way the world of entertainment works. But, I was definitely discouraged. They had a specific need and I couldn't fill it. I worked so hard to get to that point, and it was being taken away before I really got a chance to leave my mark. For the next few months I continued teaching in the training center and working corporate training sessions, but I missed the stage.

Now, this is clearly not the way I would have outlined this experience either. So, let's apply the previous formula to see how this unfolded by looking at the bigger picture and applying the "yes, and" principle.

What I thought was going to happen...

A star is born! Getting to the Main Stage cast I envisioned myself performing as long as I could. This would be my home for years which would eventually open up bigger and better doors down the road. Perhaps my dream of making it to *Saturday Night Live* weren't so far out of reach after all?

What actually happened...

My years on the Main Stage ended up being months. My rise to stardom quickly took a nose dive. Once again, I was stuck.

How I responded...

I wasn't bitter (thankfully). As I mentioned, I continued to teach in the training center and corporate sessions. I still respected and liked the two owners of the theater (and still maintain a wonderful relationship with them today). Truly, it wasn't personal, it was business. As a result of the decision my wife and I reassessed where we wanted to be. We were now parents of our first child and were growing tired of our corporate work and the cold weather. We knew at some point we wanted to live in warm weather, and this ended up being the impetus that launched us over the edge. Within months of getting let go from the Main Stage cast we packed up our things, threw a dart at a map of the Sunshine State, and moved to Jupiter, Florida.

Reflecting back…

I love looking back at this decision. The thing that made it easy for us to move from Boston to Florida was that I was able to carry my job with me. The Web site I worked for allowed me to work remotely from home, and my wife was able to find remote work as well. In the first few months of being in Florida we found our dream home at the beginning of the rise of the real estate boom. Had we waited a few months later there is no way we would have been able to afford it.

Who knows what would have happened had we stayed in Boston? Perhaps I would have auditioned for the next Main Stage cast and made it? What I do know is that shortly a year after the move I was fired from my job. In fact, my entire team was let go. Had we stayed in Boston I would of been out of a job and out of a cast, with no income coming in. In Florida I quickly connected with a local theater and co-founded an improv group with two local actors. It's been over 12 years and the three of us are still performing.

Looking back on the decision to move feels poetically planned, yet I had no idea at the time. I can still remember the hurt feelings of not getting cast on the Main Stage and asking "why is this happening?" I didn't like it, and I surely didn't agree with the decision at the time, but I knew I had a choice of how I was going to respond. I have good friends who were also not cast during that time, and some of them struggled for awhile to get back on their feet.

Similar to the St. Louis to Boston decision, this so-called setback opened yet another "yes, and" opportunity. And, as I shared earlier in the book, saying "yes, and" to getting fired from my job opened the path which eventually led to my leadership and life coaching opportunities.

Just like the victor or victim mindset that we discussed in the previous chapter, we get to choose which direction we go. Black things or red things, what are we focusing on? Each series of events can be spun into a positive or negative, and only you get to decide.

In later chapters we will discuss some helpful practices for how to better focus on the good, but the important thing to remember is that we do have a choice.

Choose wisely.

UN*STUCK* Principle #6:

Good or Bad, Who Knows?

Chapter 7:

Your Compass is Your Purpose!

If you don't know where you are going, any road will get you there. —Lewis Carroll

One of the questions I get asked all of the time is whether I have seen the film *"Yes Man"* with Jim Carrey.

I have.

Then they ask me if living "yes, and" is like that film?

Yes and no. I'll explain.

In the film, Jim Carrey's character is indeed stuck. A friend forces him to attend a motivational conference where the guru preaches saying "yes" to every opportunity, no matter what.

As you can imagine, this sends him on a crazy adventure of saying "yes" to everything from new travel destinations, a new outlook at work, to inappropriate advances from his neighbor (yeah, not a good image). He is forced well beyond his comfort zone into living life with enthusiasm and possibility.

But, it cannot be sustained. He soon realizes that you cannot say "yes" to everything. It's impossible. In desperation he kidnaps the "yes" guru and forces him to reveal the secret to living this life.

The guru is shocked that he has taken the mantra so literally, and essentially explains that the goal is not to say "yes" to everything. Instead, it is simply a tool to help people who are stuck get unstuck.

We need to say yes to the facts, but we do not and cannot say "yes" to every opportunity that comes along.

The bigger question is this…

How do I know what I should be saying "yes" to?

This is where purpose comes in. Honestly, I am a little embarrassed that it has taken seven chapters to finally address purpose because it is the basis that makes living "yes, and" possible.

If "yes, and" is the foundation of living, then your purpose is the ground it is built upon.

This chapter is all about you and your purpose.

Simon Sinek has become a household name in recent years for helping organizations and individuals understand their "why!" (I recommend you watch his TEDx talk!)

Your "why" is your reason for being.

It is not "what" you do, but "why" you do everything that you do.

Your purpose is not a thing, title, accomplishment, or activity, but rather the motivation behind all of these things.

Your purpose is untouchable. It cannot die or be stolen. It is in your heart and soul, and it can never be extinguished. Some wise teachers interchange the word "mission" for "purpose." Use whatever word you like. I will often refer to my purpose as my "YES Statement," because the word "yes" holds so much power!

Now, you (like millions of others) might be feeling like you don't know your "why." That doesn't mean it is not there. It just means it has been buried or forgotten. So, let's spend some time uncovering it.

Right now, I want you to think of the three most important things in your life. What are they?

To help, you can even write them in your book. Here is your space:

1.

2.

3.

Take a look at your three things and really ask yourself if these are the most important things in your life. Do they feel true and authentic?

Now, for each of these I want you to answer the following question...

If I were at my best, what kind of person would I be in this relationship?

When I say relationship, that can apply to a person, career, health, etc. So, for example, if one of the most important things to you is your health, you would think about what your health would look like if you were at your best.

Many of us go directly to the people in our lives. If you really want to strengthen these important relationships, I strongly encourage you to answer this question for each of them.

I did this exercise a few years back and used it to create a vision of how I would behave as a father, husband, and friend, if I were to be at my best. We want to create the ideal vision so that we have a direction to walk toward. Avoid vague language such as "be nicer" "and "do better." Instead, be specific. Describe, for example, how you want to be more patient and not get frustrated every time your child interrupts you. See yourself reacting positively in a situation that has tripped you up in the past. Articulate it, write it, and then start to create it.

If you do not know what that ideal person (you) looks like, it is a lot harder to behave at your best.

Now, using the space below, create the vision for the three most important things in your life.

1. *If I were at my best, what kind of person would I be in my* _____ *?*

2. *If I were at my best, what kind of person would I be in my _____?*

3. *If I were at my best, what kind of person would I be in my _____?*

How did that feel? It's powerful, isn't it?!

You are creating the ideal you. And when you have a vision you know which direction to walk.

Even in the world of improvisation, an improviser never walks on stage with nothing. Yes, they are creating a story on the fly, but that actor is still entering the stage with a choice. This could be anything from an emotion, physical movement, or line of dialogue, but it is something for them to work from.

Here is a scenario…

You are in Florida and I tell you that you need to get to New York. You have the option of getting a step by step map print out, or a compass.

Which would you choose?

Most of us would take the map, right? I would. Not long before Google Maps I would go to my local AAA and have them print out a "Trip Tix" for my road trip. It was essentially a booklet equivalent to what Google Maps can do in 5 seconds. (Can I tell you how old I am feel right now?)

On the other hand, the compass is helpful, but it is not going to be as efficient as using a map.

But, the night before your trip I grab you, throw you on a plane, and leave you in the middle of nowhere. Once you get over the shock of why Travis would do such a thing, how useful is your map from Florida to New York now?

What about your compass?

Yes, your compass may not be the most efficient instrument, but you can quickly figure out which direction you need to walk. The map is obsolete once you've been thrown off your path, but the compass always points to your true north.

Your compass in life is your *purpose*!

Most of us have been raised using a map. Get good grades, get into a good school, get into a better graduate school, get a good job, work your way up the ladder, get married, have kids, retire, and ride happily off into the sunset.

And, if you are like most people, this map approach to life hasn't been so simple. In fact, odds are you have been tossed and turned at different times, not sure which is up and which is down, and definitely not knowing which direction to walk.

That is precisely why we need the compass of our purpose to guide us. Our compass doesn't care what has happened to us, it still points north.

Our compass isn't concerned with the illness or getting fired, it still points north.

The compass doesn't care if you have been thrown on a plane and ushered off to a remote part of the world, it still points north.

If you zig when you were supposed to zag, your compass still points north.

No judgment. No self-condemnation. Our purpose always points us north!

The problem is most of us haven't been taught how to identify our purpose. We have bought into a prescribed version of what we are supposed to do, and who we are supposed to be, and we haven't taken the time to really mine our passions and uncover our purpose.

It's kind of silly when you think about it. Everywhere you go you see the "mission statement" plastered on the wall. Your school had a mission, your company has a mission, yet how many of us have taken the time to articulate our own mission - our purpose - our reason for being!

Not long ago I was working with a high school golfer who was struggling. He was struggling so badly that he was asking for help. Yes, you know a high schooler is struggling when they seek out help.

I am a horrible golfer, so I was relieved to find out he wasn't asking me for swing advice. What came out during our first session though is that he wasn't at peace with himself. He wasn't having fun, and he didn't like the way he was treating others. He was a wonderfully nice and pleasant guy, but he was super competitive. When he came to the academy he was very much an amateur golfer, so he always felt he needed to compete and prove himself to the coaches and other golfers. He had doubters, plenty of them, so he carried a constant chip on his shoulder.

In these competitive high-points he would say something in the heat of the moment that he would later regret. The doubts from others fueled his motivation, but it also caused him to lash out unkindly.

My goal was not to kill the competitive fire, but to help him get really clear on his motivation for playing golf. What was his "why?" What was his purpose?

His face lit up as we talked about purpose. That was it. His purpose for playing was deeply spiritual. He felt like golf was an expression of his God-given gifts. He wanted to push himself as far as he could in honor of his spirituality. Unfortunately, he was allowing himself to get distracted by the negativity of others.

I gave him the assignment of going away and creating a purpose statement for himself. When he came back the next week he was a new man. His purpose had nothing to do with beating others, but rather expressing his God-given talent. I then asked, how would you treat others if you showed up on purpose? He responded that he would be kind, positive, and encouraging.

Going through this exercise gave him a very practical framework for his behavior and actions. Whenever he reacted unlike his ideal vision of himself, he knew he was off purpose. He now knew it was just a matter of refocusing his thoughts and intentions and getting back to being the expression of his purpose.

Can you see the trap we allow ourselves to fall into by not taking the time to define who we are and what we stand for? If we're not careful, we'll wake up years down the road with the realization that we are living someone else's version of our life.

This is key in being able to "live yes, and!"

Like Jim Carrey in "*The Yes Man*," we will live like a rudderless ship when we don't have a purpose to guide us through our options. It is not about saying yes to every opportunity that comes along, but saying yes to the opportunities that fall in line with our purpose.

The brilliant Stephen Covey sums it up beautifully...

You have to decide what your highest priorities are and have the courage—pleasantly, smilingly, nonapologetically, to say "no" to other things. And the way you do that is by having a bigger "yes" burning inside. The enemy of the "best" is often the "good."

Do you know what your highest priorities are?

In my years of coaching I have worked with numerous people who feel they don't have the time to spend on the things they are truly passionate about. My response has always been...

Then what are you spending your time on?

Yes, we have jobs and responsibilities, but at the end of the day we choose how we spend our time.

I challenge all of you for the next week to keep a daily journal of how you spend every minute of your day. We believe we don't have enough time in the day to do things we love, but I will argue that the time is actually there. We just need to do a better job choosing what we are giving our time to.

As Covey mentions, we need to recognize the things that we need to say "no" to. These might be things we do out of guilt or false responsibility. They might also be mindless activities we do throughout the day that seem to take up little time. But, jumping on Facebook or Twitter 6 or 7 times a day for just 5-10 minutes ends up being more than an hour a day (And be honest, it's probably more like 10-12 times a day!)

Is there anything wrong with Facebook or Twitter? Or watching Sportscenter? Or insert any other type of activity we fall back on?

No. It is not about labeling them as a good or bad, but determining which activities support your bigger "yes!"

That is why it is so crucial to understand what your purpose is so that you can differentiate between the good and the best.

A few years back I was working with a college basketball player who would go on to play professionally for 12 years. On the court he was in the zone, but away from the game he struggled to find peace. In college, he couldn't understand why every time he would go out and party with his friends and teammates he would end up feeling guilty the next day. In his eyes, they had no problem with this lifestyle, so why did he?

Listening through this situation with him it was clear that what was good for the goose was not good for the gander. By trying to fit in, he was diminishing his own sense of purpose.

He asked me, "Why can't I party and have a good time and not feel guilty?"

My response was simply, "Because that apparently doesn't work for you."

In saying this, there is no judgment about what the other guys are doing. I am not labeling drinking and partying as a "bad" thing. But for my friend these activities clearly didn't fit in with his sense of purpose.

The opportunity for him was to more clearly define his own purpose so that he could make choices that aligned with who he wanted to be. That feeling of discomfort we get when things aren't right is actually a gift for us. It is our internal compass alerting us that we are walking in the wrong direction. The longer we walk in the wrong direction, the more uncomfortable we will become.

For millions of people on the planet, the solution for dealing with this discomfort is to ignore it, distract, or numb ourselves. If you want to live the life you are meant to live, the answer is to listen to these signals and begin walking toward your purpose. Go back to thinking about the most important things in your life and ask yourself, "Is what I am doing right now honoring the impact I want to have on the most important things in my life?"

If the answer is no, you have just discovered the source of your unrest.

If the answer is yes and you still feel unrest, you have probably identified some resistance that is challenging you from living your purpose in a bigger way. This is also a good thing. It means you are on the right path but have encountered a fear or obstacle that will stretch you outside of your comfort zone.

In her book, *When Things Fall Apart: Heart Advice for Difficult Times*, American Buddhist Pema Chodron tells this story about Buddhist meditation master Trungpa Rinpoche:

He told a story about traveling with his attendants to a monastery he'd never seen before. As they neared the gates, he saw a large guard dog with huge teeth and red eyes. It was growling ferociously and struggling to get free from the chain that held it. The dog seemed desperate to attack them. As Rinpoche got closer, he could see its bluish tongue and spittle spraying from its mouth. They walked past the dog, keeping their distance, and entered the gate. Suddenly the chain broke and the dog rushed at them. The attendants screamed and froze in terror. Rinpoche turned and ran as fast as he could—straight at the dog. The dog was so surprised that he put his tail between his legs and ran away.

When we know our purpose, and encounter fears along the way, these are dogs we run at. These are the dragons we need to slay! Sure, we can turn our back on them and hope they go away, but as soon as we return to our purpose they will be there waiting for us.

Making the decision to leave my job at the boarding school meant me running at that big dog of fear and uncertainty. Like I shared earlier, I had no plan. I just knew the time felt right. I was being impelled by my internal compass to step out of my comfort zone and walk in the direction of my authentic purpose. I didn't have a map.

Like my example, I felt like I had been plucked out of my familiar surroundings and dropped in the middle of nowhere. No one had written me a step by step map of how to navigate this situation. Instead, I had to rely on my internal compass to guide me (and the family) day by day, every step of the way. In fact, if someone had given me a map of how the following six months would unfold I would have laughed. I had no idea how I was going to defuse the fear I had running at the dog, but turning and running the other way didn't seem like an option.

I started this chapter by clarifying that living "yes, and" doesn't mean saying yes to every opportunity that comes your way. Once you understand your inner compass you will have the clarity needed to filter through the opportunities in order to choose those that align with your purpose.

A Defined Purpose = Clear Choices

Now you are able to live "yes, and!"

As life unfolds moment by moment, and we are in agreement (*yes*) with the facts, our powerful response (*and*) is easier to choose when we are grounded with our purpose.

So, instead of aimlessly letting life live us as a "yes man," we get to live life as a "Yes, And" man!

Before we move on, let's make sure we are clear on your authentic purpose. Use the space below to articulate a purpose statement for yourself that feels authentic. Remember, this is not a vision, but a purpose. A vision is an ideal goal you would love to achieve. Your purpose is who you are, your "why!" Your purpose is your service to yourself and others. My purpose is simply...

To inspire myself and others to live their brilliance through a commitment to purpose, authenticity, and life-transforming collaboration!

Your purpose is changeless (although the language may change over time).

So, take some time and the space below to write yours!

UN*STUCK* Principle #7:

Your Compass is Your Purpose!

Chapter 8:

Don't Hold Your Breath!

Transformation is my favorite game and in my experience, anger and frustration are the result of you not being authentic somewhere in your life or with someone in your life. Being fake about anything creates a block inside of you. Life can't work for you if you don't show up as you. —
Jason Mraz

Quick quiz.

You are sitting on an airplane waiting to take off and the flight attendants are walking you through what to do in case of an emergency. You are on the plane with your spouse and three kids. They flight attendant announcement proceeds…

If there is a loss in cabin pressure an oxygen mask will fall from the ceiling.

According to their instructions, who should you help with the oxygen mask first?

A) Your spouse
B) Yourself
C) Your children
D) None of the above

What is the correct answer?

D.

What? You selected "D"? What is the matter with you? Do you want everyone that you care about including yourself to die?

What?

Oh, you said "*B!*"

Sorry about that.

Of course you knew that. Everyone knows that. If you have flown a plane before you have heard the same safety instruction repeated over and over again.

Yet, whenever I fly, part of me still cringes whenever I ponder the situation. Would I really ignore my wife and kids by putting on my own mask first?

Would I have the poise in that moment to think rationally instead of emotionally?

Everyday you are essentially making the same choices; they just happen to be a little less dramatic.

The reality of putting your oxygen mask on first is that it guarantees you have what you need in order to be able to help everyone else. No matter how much you love your spouse and kids, you are of no use to them if you are selflessly unconscious. Before you can help them, you need to make sure you help yourself.

You need oxygen to breathe. You need oxygen to live!

I have worked with and delivered to countless audiences and have seen that moment of question in their eyes as they realize they are not taking the time to get their oxygen.

I have worked with organizations who put a bottom-line driven mentality over the care of the employees who deliver the service, and then not understanding why the workplace is toxic, disengaged, and apathetic. Employees need oxygen to live and be productive.

I have worked with parents, executives, and athletes who cannot figure out why they are stressed, unhappy, and stuck.

The answer in all of these situations is a symptom of the same problem…

You cannot survive, let alone excel in life, if you are always holding your breath!

We are of no use to the people we love when we are not taking care of ourselves. We are of no use to the companies we work for and the teams we serve if we are not first and foremost taking care of ourselves.

As Stephen Covey once put it, "Have you ever been making such great time on a road trip that you don't have time to stop and get gas?"

We laugh, but that is how many of us live.

"I'll get to it tomorrow."

"I'll make time this weekend."

"I will finally unwind on vacation."

Do you see how ridiculous and unsustainable this mindset is for living?

Here is the problem. We have fooled ourselves into believing that the things that bring us peace, joy, and rejuvenation are luxuries, not necessitates.

Is oxygen a luxury?

Do this for me. Use the space below to list 7-10 things that provide you with rest, joy, inspiration, relaxation, peace, etc.

*

*

*

*

*

*

*

*

*

*

Look at your list. I cannot see what you wrote down, but my guess is that it includes such things as spending time with family and friends, being in nature, being active, reading, yoga, prayer, a favorite hobby, or just having some "me" time.

We treat these as luxuries. We go on vacation where we spend time outdoors, catch up on relationships, and work on hobbies, only to abandon these activities when we return to our normal schedule.

We tell everyone how rejuvenated we feel from our vacation. Of course we are, we were doing those things that bring us joy and purpose.

We think it was simply because we were in a different location and not at work, but it is more than that. We spent time consciously (or unconsciously) connecting with our purpose and passions. We let go of day to day stress and worry, and just exhaled, surrendered, got clear...

and breathed!

We got our oxygen.

It is no surprise that I make the strong argument that these are **NOT** luxuries, they are **NECESSITIES!**

You need them to live, breathe, and be at your best! Notice how you treat those around you when you make this time for yourself. How much more patient, tolerant, present, and joyful are you when you take time for yourself?

Most of us don't think we can experience this everyday, but that is a lie.

Sure, my ideal day would be laying in a hammock on a beach with a book, spending time with my wife and kids, and then improvising at night. I cannot have that every night, but I work on bringing as much of that into my day to day as possible.

You can too.

The struggle is that we believe we need to have the beach (or whatever dream spot) in order to feel the peace and rejuvenation we get from the vacation. We also get intimidated thinking that we need to make too many major changes in our day in order to have an impact.

Both of those are untrue.

We have already discussed the need to say "no" to certain things in order to achieve your bigger "yes." That is the opportunity here.

If, for example, yoga is an activity that brings you peace and connection, how can you incorporate that into your day right now?

Most of us immediately protest that we don't have time for a 60-90 minute daily class.

I agree. So, let's start small. Do you have time for 5 minutes of yoga a day? Can you make that work?

If 5 minutes is too small, start with 10 minutes. If it's too big, start with 1 minute. Find the edge of your comfort zone and go there. Over three years ago my wife made the commitment of having a daily yoga routine. Once or twice a week she is able to get to a local yoga class. Most mornings though she wakes up, rolls out her mat, and then does anywhere from 1 minute to 30 minutes of yoga. No matter how her day unfolds she still finds even the smallest amount of time to get her oxygen. She hasn't missed a day in over 3 years!

The key is to make it a daily commitment. That is why starting small is important. All of the scientific research out there supports this as the way of creating lasting habits. Start small and build.

For over 6 years my day was filled with commitments. These were non-negotiable. If I went to bed at night and remembered that I didn't do a commitment, I would get out of bed and finish. It didn't matter if I were sick or out of town, I did my commitments.

This was a big stretch for me. As a kid I was not the type who set goals and got them done. But after attending an *Educare Learning Institute* leadership class that broke them down into smaller chunks, it became much easier.

Again, the key is to smart small. It was also recommended in the class to pick things that really resonated with your purpose. This made it a truly valuable activity. These are your oxygen activities. When I started I had 3-4 activities that took me about 10 minutes each. This felt like a good stretch outside of my comfort zone, but doable.

I committed to doing each of them a minimum of 100 days in a row. If I missed a day for that activity I would start over at day 1. This happened a few times, but I never started a commitment I didn't finish. Very quickly I realized that I was someone who could set goals and complete them. I just needed to start small and be consistent.

My 3-4 daily commitments turned into 8-10 commitments at one point. For awhile I was spending nearly 2 hours a day on my commitments. They truly were my oxygen, and despite having a job, wife, and three kids, they always got done. This also happened to come at a rough spot in my life where I needed as much oxygen as I could get.

They were fun, challenging, and they all brought me a sense of purpose. It was refreshing to know that at the end of each day I had taken time to dedicate myself to being a better person, for myself, and for everyone else. I felt it. My wife felt it. The kids felt it.

My commitments gave my day focus and intention. I most often did them in the morning as a way to establish my day, get my thoughts in the right frame of mind, and know that the most important work of my day was done. The rest was icing on the cake. My good friend Justin Sua has an expression, he calls it "Winning the morning!" My commitments were my way of winning the morning and making sure my highest work was done!

Here is a list of some of those commitments. Most were in the 10 minute range, but some definitely took longer.

- Yoga
- Prayer for my career, kids, family, etc.
- Time in nature
- Meditation
- Push-ups
- Sit-ups
- Inspiring reading
- Teaching myself how to ride a skateboard
- Running
- Blogging
- Connecting with friends

There were definitely more, but I want to tell you about two in particular that were game changers for me.

1. Juggling

Random. I know. But during this leadership class we had to do a juggling challenge - and I sucked at it!!! Here's the thing. My whole life I told myself that I couldn't juggle. It was a belief I kept in my back pocket ever since a kid and just accepted it as fact. I had seen other kids juggle with ease. I probably tried a couple of times, got intimidated, and quit. So, here I was, in my 30's, still believing I couldn't juggle.

To go back to the "victor vs. victim" mindset we talked about earlier, I had developed a victim mindset to juggling. So, to have a victor mindset, I wanted to challenge this belief.

For 10 minutes a day I committed to juggling. The first week was brutal. I was starting to believe I wouldn't be able to juggle, but I also forced myself to just stay at it and see what happens. Then there was a turning point. About two weeks in I got it. It was ugly, but I felt the rhythm. I did it. I could juggle!

Instead of quitting my commitment because I had figured it out I decided to honor the 100 day commitment. Each day I looked forward to the 10 minutes of juggling and just being present with the activity. It taught me how to relax, breathe, and focus on the moment. It became one my favorite parts of the day. In fact, I ended up keeping it as a commitment for over 120 days. Satisfied, I let it go and moved on to another commitment.

That was years ago, and now whenever I run up against something where I question my ability, I remember that I taught myself to juggle by just committing to it for 10 minutes a day.

2. The Love E-mail

I am not a sappy guy. I am a tender man, thoughtful, and not afraid to show my emotions (I tear up often on stage), but I still struggle with sharing my feelings with my wife. I love her. She knows this, but she would not call me romantic.

After hearing this idea from another person, I decided that I would write my wife an e-mail each day telling her something I love about her. Some of you might give me a hard time for using an e-mail instead of telling her, but to you people, mind your own business!

For 100 days I needed to send her something new. My wife is AMAZING! She has endless things I could say about her, but those things run out after about two weeks. 100 things! What was I thinking?

In all seriousness, it was a challenge but it wasn't hard. Now, I know my wife appreciated this commitment more than all the others. Yes, she knew I loved her, but this gave her a reminder each day. For me, it forced me to really think about her each day and see the myriad of beauty and wonderful qualities she expresses. These are the things we take for granted when we just think it, but don't share it. The actual activity of sitting down each day to write the e-mail forced me to pause, reflect, and be intentional about thinking of how much I love her.

This activity became oxygen for our marriage.

It was simple, took very little time, but man did it have an impact! I am pretty sure she still has those e-mails saved.

Over the years, all of my commitments gave me the oxygen I needed, and they continue to allow me to breathe into my fullest. When I sacrifice them, I suffer. When I ignore them, others suffer.

People often feel selfish or self-indulgent for having their commitments. You would never call a pilot selfish for getting rest in order to fly a safe plane, and you shouldn't consider your oxygen activities any less important.

So, what oxygen activities are you ready to commit to tomorrow?

1.

2.

Remember, start small and be consistent. It's not really a big deal, it just impacts every aspect of your life!

Now, let's connect your oxygen back to your purpose that we covered in the last chapter.

When you know your reason for being, you become clear on what brings you happiness and contentment. That is the direction to walk. In this chapter you have identified the oxygen activities that connect you more deeply to your purpose. When you do these activities it allows you to show up more consistently as your ideal self. Your oxygen gives you the energy and clarity to respond on purpose. When you are clear on purpose, and understand how to reinforce your purpose daily, you now have the tools to respond with "yes, and" to any situation.

It all makes sense, right?

You cannot be stuck when you are clear on the next step.

So, let's move on and put it to work!

UN*STUCK* Principle #8:

Don't Hold Your Breath!

Chapter 9:

Interrupt the Routine

Life begins at the end of your comfort zone. —Neale Donald Walsch

I love the above quote from Neale Donald Walsch. It is one of those things that we know, yet constantly resist.

Working with athletes I am continually urging them to get outside of their comfort zones. It is the only place where growth happens.

Talking to a group of baseball players I asked them to remember the first time they faced an 80 or 90 mph fastball. Most of them remembered the terror of that moment. Forget trying to get a hit. The goal was to just get out of the batter's box alive!

Then I asked them to think about the second, third, and fourth time facing that speed. Maybe they still didn't get a hit, but they were getting close. They were more relaxed, focused, and a lot less fearful. Even those who were plunked by a fastball now knew what it felt like to stand in the box and run at the dog.

What happened as a result?

The speed was the same, but they were different.

Their comfort zone had expanded.

It didn't expand by playing it safe and staying put. In order to increase your comfort zone you need to step outside of it.

Common sense, but not common practice.

Ask yourself, when is the last time you stepped outside your comfort zone?

When was it? What did you do? How did you feel?

It is probably easier to remember the last time you were pushed outside your comfort zone, not by choice. That is more common. Why? Because most of us don't willingly go beyond our comfort zone until we are pushed.

In fact, if you think about your week you can probably think of an instance where you were forced outside your comfort zone. Maybe you were asked to present something at work? Or coach your child's youth soccer team? Or deal with a difficult family ordeal?

We are constantly being asked to go beyond our comfort zone. Sometimes we choose it, sometimes it chooses us, but it is always an invitation we need to accept.

And what is our comfort zone really?

It is the familiar and expected. It is the little we think we can control. It is where we feel safe and secure. It is where we exhale and relax, and let our guard down.

It is...comfortable.

It is also boring, stagnant, and let's be honest, it is delusional. In our comfort zone we buy into the illusion that we can control our situation, our surroundings, and others. It is where we resist change. And if there is one constant in life (in addition to death) it is that everything is constantly changing. Every relationship, marketplace, weather condition, and cell on your body is constantly changing.

It is our desire to have a comfort zone that is actually the cause of our discomfort. (Come on, I give you permission to tweet that.) When you look closely enough to any pain, stress, or anxiety in your life it is the result of resisting change. Life is screaming at you to say "yes, and" and accept the facts, yet you are holding on for dear life to what was. Who is going to win that battle?

There is absolutely nothing wrong with your comfort zone, unless you are against growing. That's all.

Living "yes, and" allows you to get out of your comfort zone willingly, not because you are an extreme thrill seeker, but because you understand the constancy of change. You are not surprised by it because you expect it.

Rocky Balboa is a great example of this. (No, Stallone did not pay for the reference, yet.) Think back to *Rocky IV*. Drago has just killed Apollo Creed prompting Rocky out of retirement to defend his friend's death. Not even Adrian thinks Rocky can win the fight. So what does Rocky do? He schedules the fight in Russia, as far out of his comfort zone as possible. He then rents a small house in the middle of Siberia and begins training with nothing but snow, mountains, a barn, and farm equipment. While Drago trains with state of the art technology (and steroids), Rocky trains in candlelit solitude and boots.

The movie begins with Rocky living an extreme life of comfort and luxury (especially for the 80's) with his mansion, giant swimming pool, Ferrari, and talking robot. The message is clear. The comfortable life has made him soft, weak, and vulnerable. In order to respond to this insurmountable challenge he must go back to what made him successful in the first place... discomfort and struggle.

We know the ending. Rocky wins, ends the Cold War (thank you Stallone), and reminds us that, "If I can change, and you can change, than we all can change!" Come on, does it get any better than that?

By choosing to go outside of our comfort zone we eliminate the shock of surprise. This is how elite military divisions prepare their soldiers to be able to respond calmly and clearly to any obstacle or challenge that arises in combat.

Tom Spooner is a retired United States Army Special Forces operator. He is also the co-founder of *Mission 22, Elder Heart,* and *Warriors Heart.* All three organizations were started as the result of his own personal struggles with PTSD and TBI (traumatic brain injury) and chemical dependency. The purpose of *Mission 22* is to raise awareness, enlist support, and end veteran suicide in America. The purpose of *Warriors Heart* is to provide a place for Veterans and first responders to heal with dignity and respect.

Tom knows all about being in the heat of the battle beyond his comfort zone, yet being able to rely on his training to respond effectively to the situation. He shared this with me:

The element of surprise and unpredictability is what throws most of us for a loop. This is one of the reasons United States Army Special Operations training is so intense, demanding, and unpredictable. One of the goals is to get the soldiers so far out of their comfort zones during training that they are able to respond to any situation. Through this training methodology, they will obtain the ability to be comfortable in uncomfortable situations. The motto "Selection is an ongoing process" becomes their culture. Being individually tested everyday becomes the norm.

I love that, "Being individually tested everyday."

It is our routine that is dangerous. Routine creates a sense of "normalcy" that doesn't really exist. We all get fooled into thinking that we like the normal, but that is not true. Normal is boring. What we really want to know is that we will be financially stable, healthy, and that our loved ones are safe.

After that, we crave adventure. We want twists, turns, and surprises. We go to movies because we want to be entertained by the unexpected. We want to be inspired by the hero's journey. Why? Because we see slices of ourselves in those characters. When that normal is broken, how do they respond? How would we respond in a similar situation?

As an improviser my goal is to find and create the unexpected. Routine is death on stage. It is boring. In fact, improvisers have a term for doing this in a scene. It is the name of this chapter.

Interrupt the Routine.

In an improvised scene, the actors involved are trying to get on the same page as quickly as possible using "yes, and." The reason for getting on the same page is so that they can work together with a common understanding of the who, what, where, why, and how details of the scene. They want to establish the facts. This is intentional. Then, once the facts are established, and the audience thinks they know where the scene is going, the improvisers take it in a new direction. This unexpected twist allows for new creativity and exploration to evolve - while keeping the audience on the edge of their seats.

Think of it as Disney World's Space Mountain. If you have never ridden Space Mountain, spoiler alert, it's fun! As old as it is it still is an awesome thrill because the whole ride takes place in pitch black. You know there is going to be another turn or drop, but you literally can't see it coming. It is hard to see your own hand in front of your face.

In an improvised scene, the same is true. It is filled with twists and turns, and as soon as the audience thinks they know where it's going, you throw them another twist. It's the same reason we love mysteries. We want to be surprised.

But it is one thing to go to an amusement park or movie where we are inviting surprises, compared to the uninvited curveballs we experience in our day to day lives. We know they are going to happen, yet we trick ourselves into trying to keep everything as it is… changeless.

It's impossible. Everything is always changing. As soon as we get comfortable with our life routine, you can guarantee it is going to get interrupted.

"Not now."

"Why me?"

"Why now?"

We have all felt this way. There is no good timing for some of these unseen events. The difference is being able to embrace a "yes, and" mindset that not only expects the interruptions, but actually invites them.

Even when it comes to my daily commitments, I am aware that the goal is not to get comfortable, but rather engage in activities that are stretching me and mentally keeping me on my toes.

Great creatives have known this forever. You know it too, you just don't know you know it. We say things like, "I just need to clear my head," or "We need to look at this with fresh eyes."

What you are really saying is that you need to interrupt the routine. You need to come at the situation from a different perspective. You need to be open to the new or illogical.

The best improvised scenes are often provoked by a mistake from one of the actors. Mispronouncing a simple word, forgetting someone's name, or not knowing common information opens up the scene to go in a direction that couldn't have been planned or foreseen. If the actors are not comfortable with mistakes they may get flustered and allow the scene to spiral downward. Experienced improvisers, on the other hand, come alive when a mistake is made. In fact, they don't see it as a mistake at all but rather an opportunity to create a scene that has never been created before.

Instead of getting tripped up with the mistake, or ignoring it, they "yes, and" the idea and turn it into comedy genius (most of the time).

The unexpected twist is what makes the scene interesting. Great improvisers know how to do this naturally by taking scenes in unconventional directions and finding brilliance. You have that same ability, even if you never demonstrate it on stage.

One of the athletes I worked with on the United States Under 17 National Soccer Team broke his leg in August, roughly seven months before the World Cup qualifying tournament. You can imagine his disappointment when he thought about the timing of his injury and his chances of making the final roster.

When the time came to choose the final roster for the qualifiers, he was on it. Not only did he make the team, he went on to score multiple goals and become a real leader for the squad during their successful qualification campaign. One of his teammates complimented his ability to strike the ball effectively with both feet, which he attributed to the time he spent working with his opposite leg while his broken leg recovered.

What seemed so unfortunate at the moment actually turned into a greater blessing down the road. His routine was interrupted with the broken leg, and it led him to a place he would not have chosen otherwise. He didn't have to like the fact that he was injured, but instead of wallowing and feeling sorry for himself he said "yes, and" and turned the setback into a strength.

Coca-Cola and Pepsi, plastic, Goodyear, Rogaine, Viagara, microwave ovens, Silly Putty, Play-Doh, and Penicillin were all created as mistakes. They are the result of science and research working on one project or goal, only to have a new discovery come as a result. [2]

---

[2] (SOURCE: http://www.thestreet.com/story/11122700/11/17-products-that-were-invented-by-accident.html)

Looking at that list, I am sure you can find one or more things you are grateful for, right fellas?

Now, for yourself, think about a time when the unexpected led to an awesome new journey or opportunity.

What happened? What were you working on that took an unexpected twist? What setback led you in a new direction?

Can you look back and connect the dots in reverse, seeing the good that came as an interruption to your routine?

Whatever happened, it was your ability to say "yes, and" to the situation that moved you forward. So, why don't we do this more consciously?

We can. Remember, our routine is going to be interrupted whether we like it or not, so let's get ahead of the curve.

The reason change is so uncomfortable is because we get attached to our stories and expectations. Just like we need to constantly examine our beliefs on whether they are helping us respond as a victor or victim, we need to examine our mental attachments as well.

Ask yourself, what things in your life are you strongly attached to not changing?

Again, you will probably think about relationships and health not wanting to change. That makes sense. But, are you willing to ponder the possibility (and probability) that they will change. They have no choice. I am not saying they are going to change for the better or worse, in fact it is probably both. The thing to accept is that they will change.

So, as they change, are you open to changing with them? Guess what? You will be changing too. The thoughts, feelings, and beliefs you have right now will be different tomorrow, and probably much more different a few years from now.

What we need to do is develop the ability to keep fresh eyes. Children view the world with awe and possibility, and as things change they adapt and change with them. I am not saying a child is not capable of a cosmic meltdown and temper tantrum, but observe how quickly they are able to move on and let things go.

It is the attachment that causes the pain.

"Attachment to what?"

Attachment to anything. A person, a physical object, an outcome. We don't see it as attachment, but it is. It shows up in our goals and expectations to the extent that we struggle to deal with "what is," because we are so attached to "what we think it should be!"

You look at your spouse and get upset with their behavior because they don't behave the way "you" want them to behave. You get frustrated with your career because you don't progress or get compensated the way "you" feel you should be rewarded. You go on vacation and complain about the weather because it doesn't unfold the way "you" had hoped.

If you strip away your expectations from all of these situations you are simply left with "what is." Instead, you waste your energy and exhaust others around you with your unfair life.

A few years back my wife and I scored tickets to see Oprah Winfrey live in St. Louis for a taping of her *Life Class* program. Iyanla Vanzant, the world renowned author and life coach, was her featured guest that day and she shared an idea that has stuck with me ever since.

Iyanla is a master at identifying the victim mindset with the clients she works with. During her talk she broke it down this way. Since I was there live, this is essentially how I remember it.

We experience every event in three ways:

1)   *The facts.* These are the physical details of what happened. If you were in a car accident. The facts are that you were in a car accident, as well as the physical details of the event.

2)   *The story.* The story is what you create as a result of the facts. You take the facts and give them meaning. You can create whatever story you choose. "The world is out to get me!" "They were driving too fast." "I will never feel safe again." You can also have positive stories, "Well, accidents happen. I am glad I am okay." "It's just a car." "I guess I need to pay better attention next time." So many stories, and we are the ones who create them.

3)   *The Truth.* For Iyanla, she takes this to a spiritual depth that I happen to believe in myself. This points to what you believe in your heart about life and Spirit. The Truth, as Iyanla shares it is that no matter what happens, you are still safe in Love. You can never be outside of Love.

Whether or not you choose to believe in the spirituality of the third point, points one and two are enough to rock your world. We cannot control what happens, but we can and do create the story.

The story you create comes from your beliefs. There they are again. Your beliefs influence your behavior and create your habits. Your stories and attachments are the direct result of your beliefs. If the stories you create are rich with drama and victimization, it is because you are still attached to limiting beliefs. As the late and marvelous Wayne Dyer often said,

If you change the way you look at the things, the things you look at change.

Living "yes, and" is about letting go of being attached to outcomes, and saying "yes" to the facts. Once we say yes we can then choose an "and" response authentically connected to our purpose.

People often think that I am advocating accepting tough situations, and therefore accepting a rough plight in life. I am ABSOLUTELY not saying that.

Just the opposite. I am encouraging people to say yes to the facts, and then responding with authority built on purpose. It is your story. You are the author; therefore you have authority!

A few years back I was introduced to John O'Leary. You may know John because of his podcast or his national best-selling book *"On Fire: The 7 Choices to Ignite a a Radically Inspired Life."* John has become a dear friend and a mentor of mine in the world of public speaking. John is love and integrity in action. His *LAUNCH* leadership conferences are a shot in the arm (and heart) to anyone in a leadership position (which, as we know, is everyone).

As a 9 year-old boy John was playing with fire in his garage when the gas can he was holding exploded and blew him twenty feet into the wall. When he stood up he was covered in gasoline and flames. He ran into his home on fire where his sisters and older brother worked for over five minutes to beat off the flames. By the time John arrived at the hospital over 95% of his body was badly burned. He was given less than 1% chance to live through the night.

To hear John share his story is moving. I have had the honor to hear him share it more than once, and each time I am moved to tears. That first night in the hospital John asked him mom if he was going to die? Her response was powerful.

She asked John, "Do you want to die?"

John said "no."

His mom then responded, "Then John, you need to work harder than you've ever worked before!"

John's mother gave him a choice. She couldn't change the facts of what had happened. A horrible event had occurred. But the facts don't determine the outcome. The outcome is a future event, not the present moment. In the present moment we have the ability to respond with all of the authority available to us.

In that moment John chose life. In doing so he was forced to challenge death and grave predictions on a daily basis for months. The battle was long and painful, but day to day, moment by moment, John didn't let the facts of the situation dictate his outcome.

That is living "yes, and!"

Facts don't make us a victim, it is our response to the facts that determine the outcome.

As I mentioned, I am honored to have John as a friend in my life. His life is an example of living "yes, and." Last year I gave him a sign that reads "yes, and." It hangs in his *Rising Above* corporate offices, and he told me recently that his team incorporates the idea of "yes, and" into every meeting.

We will not choose the majority of the adversity that comes our way. But the one thing we know for sure, they will come.

Instead of sitting back, closing our eyes, and hoping that the adversity never arrives, we can be proactive in noticing the fears and attachments we have created. When we are aware of the fears and attachments we can either choose to explore them and consciously interrupt the routine, or not.

Regardless, with or without your consent the routine will be interrupted. The question is, will you play the role of the victim, or respond with the authority of your "yes, and?"

It's your choice!

UN*STUCK* Principle #9:

Interrupt the Routine

Chapter 10:

Turn Competition into Collaboration

Well, you are about to start the greatest improvisation of all. With no script. No idea what's going to happen, often with people and places you have never seen before. And you are not in control. So say "yes." And if you're lucky, you'll find people who will say "yes" back. —Stephen Colbert

A few years back I attended a talk by two former track athletes who shared a message of how they pushed each other to successes they never could have achieved on their own. The beautiful thing about their story is that not only were the two men best friends, they were also rivals.

As track and field decathletes, the two met while competing against each other at small colleges in the midwest. Fierce competitors on the track, off the track the two quickly became friends. After college they decided to move to California together to train in hopes of making the Olympics. During those few years of training and competing together they each set single event decathlon world records.

Both of them shared how setting a world record would not have been possible had the other not been there pushing them. Each day they tried to kill each other on the track. It was the competition that pushed them to new heights. Although both of them came up short qualifying for the Olympic Games, they both feel they reached their full potential.

Years later, and a few timezones away, a middle school boy moved to northern Michigan. Basketball was his passion. Within days of being in his new small-town he met the local kid who dominated the basketball court. A rivalry was born. Amidst this passion of trying to destroy each other on the court the two forged a bond. On the court, it was war. Off the court, they were inseparable. In high school they became local legends. Home and away games were sold-out to see the small-town basketball duo.

One would go on to set an NAIA scoring record in his college conference. The other would be the first player from the small-town of Petoskey to receive an NCAA Division I athletic scholarship. He would lead his team to three NCAA tournament appearances, including a trip to the Elite 8. After a few near miss NBA try-outs he went on to enjoy a successful 13-year professional career in Europe. Yet, without the competition that began back in middle school, none of it would have been possible.

I think most of us have the wrong idea when we think of competition. We have turned it into a bad word. I myself have questioned the value of sports at times seeing what competition brings out in players, parents, and fans. We have taken it from its true essence of expressing our highest potential and inspiring others, to a selfish, "me first" mentality based on ego and personal gain.

But when you look at competition from the perspective of the two examples above, it has a different meaning. It is pure. It is compassionate. It is about motivating others beyond what they can do on their own, helping them achieve their potential while also pushing yourself to new heights. On our own, it is a lot easier to take shortcuts. But when you have someone else training beside you, pushing you, motivating you, it brings out another level of possibility.

To me, competition in its purest form is actually *cooperation*.

On stage as an improviser, the goal is cooperation. You cannot compete on stage as an improviser and have the end result be anything enjoyable. No one wants to watch a battle of wills on stage between two performers. The misconception is that in order to have cooperation you need to be passive. A passive improviser is an out of work improviser.

A seasoned improviser knows that their job is to make strong choices and provide ideas in order to give their partner information to work with. The goal of an improviser is to bring ideas, energy, and confidence to the stage, and then find a way to integrate with the other performers who are also doing the same. The end result is a scene where ideas and creativity are being matched with more ideas and creativity. It is the ability to feel the diversity of the whole symphony working together in unison, compared to a group of individual musicians all doing their own thing.

Collaboration is about combining and interweaving ideas in a way that creates something where everyone contributes and benefits to an extent that cannot be achieved individually.

Stephen Covey (not to be confused with Stephen *Colbert*) would have called it a "win-win" situation. Like the athletes mentioned above, their competition with one another resulted in a collaboration where each benefited, including the team as a whole.

Conversely, when most of us think of a competition it is from the standpoint of trying to find our own success through the defeat or demise of another. We see it as a "win-lose" scenario.

So what is it that makes seeing a "win-win" outcome so difficult? For whatever reason, nature or nurture, societal reasons, etc., most of us turn collaborative "win-win" opportunities into competitive "win-lose" or "lose-lose" results.

Being stuck can feel like a "win-lose" or "lose-lose" situation. Our options seem limited, and instead of feeling connected to a group of supporters, we feel isolated.

One of my favorite activities is to bring up a group of volunteers and split them into two teams. I then "hand" them an imaginary rope and challenge them to a contest of tug-of-war. It is always interesting to see what happens. Usually both teams will battle back and forth, and since there really isn't a rope, it looks as if both teams are winning. Sometimes this goes on for awhile. The imaginary rope gets stretched in both directions, and both teams declare they won. It's awkward.

We then talk about the activity and ask why neither team wanted to lose? Think about it, it's imaginary tug-of-war. Losing at "make believe" shouldn't be so damaging to our ego, but it is. Even in a situation where "winning" has no reflection of our worth, we still can't let it go.

Once in a great while you will have two teams battle, and then almost as if working from a script, one team will let go of the rope and fall back in defeat. They console each other while the other team cheers in victory. It's quite a scene to see and so much more entertaining than watching two egos battle each other.

The ego loves to compete as an excuse for protecting its own insecurity. That is the only reason you would ever care whether or not you won an imaginary tug-o-war battle.

When competition becomes solely about individual success and gain, regardless of what happens to anyone else, it then becomes a dirty word.

What we need instead is competition from the standpoint of the "win-win" mindset, which ultimately turns into collaboration. If I am committed to giving my best effort (whether you are my teammate or my opponent) it causes you to bring your best effort. As a result, we both grow and improve. But, if one of us decided to take it easy on the other, it actually ends up hurting us both. So, my goal as your competitor is not to humiliate you, but rather respect your growth by giving you the best that I have.

The best articulation of competition I have ever read is from Timothy Gallwey in his book *The Inner Game of Tennis*. Gallwey uses the analogy of the surfer who wants to become the best he can be. In order to do so he must continually seek out bigger waves that will challenge him. The waves, although menacing, are there to promote the surfer's growth by the challenge they present. Instead of the wave being his enemy, he treats it as his biggest ally for growth.

Gallwey writes:

Once one recognizes the value of having difficult obstacles to overcome, it is a simple matter to see the true benefit that can be gained from competitive sports. In tennis, who is it that provides a person with the obstacles he needs in order to experience his highest limits? His opponent, of course! Then is your opponent a friend or an enemy? He is a friend to the extent that he does his best to make things difficult for you. Only by playing the role of your enemy does he become your true friend. Only by competing with you does he in fact cooperate. It's the duty of your opponent to create the greatest possible difficulties for you, just as it is yours to try to create obstacles for him. Only by doing this do you give each other the opportunity to find out to what heights each can rise.

You may remember earlier in the book when I said, *"You cannot progress until you say yes!"*

You need to say "yes" to the current situation in order to make progress. When we feel stuck it is because we are in competition with the current moment, thus making it the enemy. It is not the enemy, good or bad (who knows), it is simply what is happening right now. Instead of competing with it, say "yes" and cooperate with it as quickly as possible.

Yes, And!

The same goes with conflict. In the example of the tug-of-war, the team that allowed themselves to lose did so for the benefit of the activity. It was so much more interesting than seeing two teams pull at an imaginary rope for 5 minutes. By saying "yes" to losing, they allowed the overall situation to progress.

Losing in real life is often just accepting what is happening. Again, we don't need to like it, but as long as we are resisting it we are not allowing progress to take place. Embracing the next moment leaves us open to solutions we can't find while dwelling on the past.

You cannot progress until you say yes!

Nick Vujicic has inspired millions. Born with no arms or legs, Vujicic's full life and adventurous spirit has led him to places and experiences that far exceed any "disability." In his book "Life Without Limits," Nick shares his wisdom and brilliance for what it means to collaborate with what life gives you instead of being in conflict and competition with the facts:

"Some injuries heal more quickly if you keep moving. The same is true of setbacks in life. Perhaps you lose your job. A relationship might not work out. Maybe the bills are piling up. Don't put your life on hold so that you can dwell on the unfairness of past hurts. Look for ways instead to move forward. Maybe there is a better job awaiting you that will be more fulfilling and rewarding. Your relationship may have needed a shake-up, or maybe there is someone better for you. Perhaps your financial challenges will inspire you to find new creative ways to save and build wealth."

"Keep moving." I love that. Life is always happening in the present moment. Right now! So, instead of getting stuck with 30 seconds ago, 3 weeks ago, or 3 years ago, keep moving and begin collaborating with this moment.

I want you to think about a relationship you are challenged with right now.

Do you have someone in mind?

What is it about the relationship that is difficult?

My wife and I have been married for almost 20 years, and in that time we have had a few bumpy days. Without fail, each rift in our marriage has been the result of turning our relationship into a competition.

Think about your wedding vows for a second. My assumption is that if you boiled your wedding vows down to their essence they would center around selflessness and unconditional love. Am I wrong? (If not, I really want to see your vows.)

Selflessness and unconditional love. These are two pretty common qualities for a successful marriage. Not always very easy though.

Does anyone have wedding vows based on lists of what your spouse needs to do *for* you? Do your wedding vows include keeping score and making sure you both do an equal amount of work all of the time?

Probably not.

But that is often what we do. Like most other areas of our life, we turn our most sacred relationships into competitions.

Not collaboration.

When you said "yes" on your wedding day, you didn't know you were also saying "yes, and!"

That is what a healthy relationship is built on…

Collaboration.

Instead we make mental lists of all of the things we are doing compared to the other person. We want them to behave the way *we* want them to act, and when they don't we find reasons for how they need to be better. In fact, we tell them all of the ways we are fulfilling our end of the bargain and how they are not.

Selflessness and unconditional love?

Nope. In fact, we often put a whole lot of conditions on our love. We consciously and unconsciously say,

"If you behave this way, I will behave this way, and we will be happy."

Deal. Great!

Collaboration doesn't work that way. It doesn't keep score. It is not conditional.

A healthy relationship cannot be based on only giving love when the other person does what we want. That is not love. That is convenience and manipulation.

In improvisation we use a mantra…

Make your partner look like a genius!

When you take the stage your goal and focus is on your partner. Your goal is to make them look good. You listen to their ideas, accept them, support them, and then build off of them. Here is the kicker, their goal is to make YOU look like a genius. So while you are focusing on them, they are focusing on you. Both of you are active participants, both of you have ideas, and both of you are working on celebrating the other person. Imagine how good that is going to look on stage.

Now, take that same mantra into your relationships. What if your goal today is to make your spouse feel like a genius? What if your goal as a parent is to make your child feel supported? What if your goal as a teacher is to make your students feel brilliant? What if your goal as a coach is to make your players feel incredible? What if your goal as a manager, CEO, or executive is to make your employees feel amazing and valued?

What if we treated each other like people instead of opponents?

What if we cooperated instead of competed?

There have been days (fewer than desired) when I have come home from work with the mindset that I am going to ask my wife what I can do to help her. You see, not only is she the primary homeschooler for our three kids, she also keeps our home organized, balances our finances, and works about 20-30 hours a week as a freelance customer service representative (and she is a photographer).

As you can see, if I were keeping score with my wife I would lose every time. So, if I were to come home and get annoyed with having to work on a project, or do an errand for her, or complain about all the work I did that day, it easily could escalate into an argument about who is doing what. It becomes a competition.

Now, for all of you married people out there, I know you are nodding while you read this. If you cannot relate to this, put the book down, you are done!

Again, think of the relationship I asked about earlier. Can you find an element of that relationship where there may be some competition taking place? Odds are the other person is letting you down with the way they are showing up.

If it's a child, you may perceive them not treating you with the appreciation you feel you deserve. With a spouse you may feel they are not contributing to the family as much as you. With a friend you may think they take advantage of you, and don't give the same time in return. With a co-worker you may feel they are not upholding their end of the bargain.

Whatever the relationship, can you find how you may have slipped into a competition mindset?

You are stuck.

So, what if you flipped into a collaboration mindset? What if instead of asking…

What can they do for me?

You asked…

How can I support their cause or needs today?

How can you help them look and feel like a genius today?

When I do this, it works wonders! It is not a technique - it is a mindset, it is unconditional love.

Keeping score is about winning. Relationships are NOT competitions. The challenge with marriage, like any relationship, or anything in the world, is that it is constantly changing. The person you married is different than the person you are now married to. That is not meant to be scary, it's just reality. You are not the person you were when you got married. Thank God! Look how much you have grown, matured, learned, and evolved since saying "I do!" Your partner is no different.

Marriage is the ultimate "yes, and" agreement. You show up with all of your "stuff" and your partner shows up with all of their "stuff," and you throw them together and make them work. It is not about compromise, it's collaboration! When you get married you don't just marry the good qualities in the other person - you get all of them. It is your ability to embrace the good and the bad that allows the relationship to grow.

As a parent, there is no greater arena for challenging your "yes, and" mindset. In fact, this phrase came out of my 12-year old daughter's mouth more than once, "For someone who teaches "yes," you sure like to say "no!" That one stung a little.

But it's true. As much as we want to be our kids biggest cheerleaders and support all of their dreams and ideas, it is really hard to keep our opinions and judgments out of the way. Really hard!!!

Yet, as the parent you have the largest impact on developing this mindset in your child. What you say, and more importantly, how you behave, will serve as either a positive or negative example for your child to learn from. Your child, more than anything else, wants your acceptance. They want to feel like you understand them, that you "get them." You don't even need to like the same things that they like, but are you able to support and champion their passions? Can you do so without judgment? Can you do so without making them feel "less than" for not liking what you like?

One of the ways my wife and I have tried to nurture the "yes, and" mindset with our kids is by allowing them to have a voice and choice. As difficult as it is to get constant opinions from our kids, we want them to feel that their ideas matter and are heard. Even if we can't do what they like, we want them to know that they matter. And, at times it is great when we can collaborate ideas and create win-win situations for everyone.

As I mentioned earlier in the book, I often think about what my children are going to say about me as a father on their wedding day. What is the influence and impact I had on their lives? Did I support their passions and purpose? Did I love them unconditionally? Did I help them live their "yes, and?"

Did I compete with their desires, or did I collaborate with them in finding their brilliance?

Was I a "yes, and" father?

Like the other principles, recognizing the difference between a competition and collaboration mindset is a game changer. I use it as a trigger. When I feel myself slipping into a competition frame of mind I can feel it in my body. It awakes the opportunity in me to switch into collaboration or continue on the painful path of competition.

If you are stuck, stop competing with where you are and what you are doing. Stop fighting with what is.

Look up. Look around. There is opportunity in this moment. Instead of noticing everything you don't like about your situation, accept the facts and keep moving. Stop seeing obstacles as enemies and turn them into allies. Stop treating your relationships like competitions and transform them into partnerships. Stop seeing your employees as "us vs. them" and change it to "we." Stop seeing yourself as separate from everything and everyone else, and begin collaborating.

The world is not out to get you. So go out and get the world!

<u>UN*STUCK* Principle #10:</u>

Turn Competition into Collaboration

The 3 Words and 10 Principles for Getting Unstuck

3 words: *Live Yes, And!*

10 Principles

1. The Answer to "How" is "Yes!"

2. Life is the Performance

3. There are No Mistakes

4. Embrace the Goo

5. Belief It

6. Good or Bad, Who Knows?

7. Your Compass is Your Purpose

8. Don't Hold Your Breath

9. Interrupt the Routine

10. Turn Competition into Collaboration

Conclusion:

The "Yes, And" Life!

You are in the process of writing your life story, and no good story is without a hero or heroine overcoming their fair share of challenges. In fact, the bigger the challenges, the better the story. Since there are no restrictions and no limits to where your story goes from here, what do you want the next page to say? —Hal Elrod

The idea for this book was born on experience and time. It was the book I always wanted to write, I just needed to go out and experience it for myself and meet others who have done the same.

Near the completion of the book I was reunited with a young woman who was one of my leadership summer workers while at IMG. I told her about the book and the message and then it dawned on me how perfectly her story is to the "yes, and" narrative.

Her name is Alyssa and her passion growing up was gymnastics. Years of competing at a high level took a toll on her body, even as a child. Before even getting to college she had already endured three ACL injuries and surgeries. Within her first few months as a college Division I gymnast she suffered her fourth ACL injury. She was devastated.

The doctor asked her if she wanted to still be able to walk when she was 30? If so, she needed to stop gymnastics. The decision was obvious, but not easy. While going through rehab for her knee she was approached by the college diving coach. Although she hadn't done any diving since being a young child the coach believed her air awareness would translate to diving. After a full year of rehab, and learning a new sport, she finished her last two years of college as an NCAA Division I diver.

"Yes, and!" Alyssa then enrolled at Florida State University for graduate school where she learned about the FSU Circus Program. As a gymnast and diver Alyssa had amazing body control and strength, the perfect combination for performing the flying trapeze, silks, and Spanish Web. Although she never imagined being a circus performer, her ability to respond to life with a "yes, and" mindset opened new doors and opportunities. It may have not been the adventure she planned, but it ended up being a lot more fun and interesting.

Alyssa lives "Yes, And!"

My good friend Evan has been an inspiration for me for many years. We first connected around 2005 as neighbors and quickly became friends. He and his wife owned and managed an art studio in Palm Beach Gardens. They lived in a beautiful house, the business was doing well, and life for the most part was generally stress free.

Then 2007 happened.

Overnight the art business in Palm Beach disappeared. Most of the other art galleries in the area closed shop. It was clear this recession wasn't going to be a quick one. Evan and his wife needed to make some tough decisions.

They cut staff so that is was just the two of them, but that wasn't enough. No one had disposable income to buy art. Evan had to do more, and that meant considering the unthinkable. They decided to sell their dream house.

They downsized their stuff, and with their young son, the three of them moved into a small townhouse. The art gallery was hemorrhaging money, and debt was growing out of control. Declaring bankruptcy seemed like the right choice, but Evan was led to hold on. With no one buying art he stayed open to other opportunities. One demand that arose was the need for art to be transported across the country. Evan owned an art moving van, so with a big hearty "yes, and" he would spend weeks at a time on the road away from the family delivering art. It wasn't much, but it was something.

Along the way something new opened up inside Evan. Whether it was the time to reflect while on the road or being forced so far outside of his comfort zone - a new sense of peace was found.

I knew Evan during this whole time while I was going through my own financial crisis. Yet, through all of it, Evan remained steady. This was clearly not the journey he thought he signed up for, but this is what he was getting, and he was responding with a powerful "yes, and!"

To date, the art gallery remains. Debt is still being paid off, but the business has stabilized. Through it all, Evan and his wife have remained positive (incredibly positive) and joyous. They are the kind of people you look forward to being around because they make everyone and everything feel okay. And most recently Evan shared with me that the gallery had its biggest month of business ever!

Evan just also happens to be one of my biggest cheerleaders. Even during the times when I really had no idea what light (if any) was at the end of my tunnel, Evan was always there with his permanent smile urging me along. Despite going through his own difficult struggles, he always had time to share his love and support.

Evan lives "Yes, And!"

As I have detailed plenty in this book, I have tried to model my own life in the "yes, and" spirit. It happens every time I run into traffic on the road, experience an unforeseen inconvenience, or find myself dealing with a more dramatic and scary personal event.

In those moments of fear, confusion, and frustration - I hear "yes, and" whispering in my head. Sometimes I wish I could shut it off, and other times I just want to ignore it, but it is always there.

When I finally come around to accepting what is happening, my response is often obvious. It's responding on purpose in the present moment, each moment, every moment. Simple, but not easy.

My favorite analogy that I have used over the years is that of the thermometer and the thermostat. The thermometer is an instrument that tells you the temperature of the outside environment. The thermostat is an instrument used to control the temperature of the environment.

Which would you rather be?

Unfortunately, it is easy to respond to life as the thermometer. Your level of happiness and disappointment rises and falls based on everything going on around you. You allow yourself to get sucked into the drama. Good external events make you happy. Bad external events cause you grief.

Conversely, the thermostat is like the image of the monk deep in meditation. Cool, calm, collected. The thermostat sets the temperature instead of letting the outside forces control it. So, despite all of the drama, or excitement going on from moment to moment, having a thermostat disposition means that you stay in your zone. Emotionally you don't experience many peeks and valleys. As the elements around you get hot or cold, you can stay at a comfortable 72 degrees (or whatever temperature works for you).

I used to think that having this kind of attitude would mean living a boring life. Let's be honest, drama is exciting! It can make us feel alive with passion, anger, and intensity. There is nothing sexy about staying calm and neutral in every situation. Right?

Neutral. That is what staying calm looked like to me. I didn't want to be neutral. No one tunes into a reality show to see everyone get along with one another. No one watches the news to see what "didn't" happen today. For me, to be calm meant not caring. So, what about those times when amazing things happen? Neutrality would keep me from really experiencing that ecstasy.

But I was wrong. Being a thermostat, staying calm, does not mean staying neutral. The drama is in the attachment. Our excitement rises when the outcome matches or exceeds our expectations, and we are disappointed when it doesn't.

Like the farmer and his son…*"Good or bad, who knows?"*

Hopefully this book has detailed that living with a "yes, and" mindset is not about being neutral, but being so fully alive and engaged with every experience that you celebrate each moment by being in collaboration with it. You can't be neutral and apathetic and live "yes, and." Responding with a "yes, and" mindset requires enthusiasm, passion, and intention! There is nothing neutral about those qualities.

A few years back I was the assistant coach for a college soccer team. Early on in preseason training I gave a talk to the young men about taking responsibility for their experience. I didn't know it at the time, but it became the theme most talked about throughout the season.

The idea I addressed was authority.

What do you think of when you think of authority? A parent, teacher, boss, judge, or law enforcement? These are the images that typically come to mind.

It was a word I hadn't given much thought to most of my life. Despite being an English major and having to

...ble in words quite often, I never really examined the root word of authority.

Author!

That is the root word. Duh, right?

So, to be in a position of authority essentially means that we are "authoring" our experience. What does an author do? An author creates and dictates how the story is going to be told. When you have authority you have control. You get to call the shots.

As I spoke to these young men I reminded them that the season was theirs to define and write. Sure, there were going to be lots of distractions and obstacles along the way, but at the end of the day, you are the author. It is your story. What are you going to write?

This is the same question I pose to you.

What is your story going to look like? Do you like what you have authored so far? What are the obstacles, distractions, and illusions preventing you from writing out the biggest, baddest, and fiercest life you can imagine?

This is living "yes, and!"

Being an author doesn't mean that you get to control the events of your life, but you ALWAYS control how you respond. That is powerful. Think of it this way, life is essentially the best creative partner you could have. Instead of trying to figure out the entire story on your own, life is there beside you to throw out events and experiences that you then get to respond to. That is where the fun and adventure comes in.

How are you going to respond when life throws you a curve ball?

Author your response. Live, "yes, and!"

Jim Carrey gave one of the most powerful and thoughtful commencement addresses to the 2014 Maharashi University graduating class. He describes his path to following his heart after watching his dad sacrifice his passion in order to take the safe and responsible path to provide for his family. Unfortunately, he got laid-off from his safe job and the family struggled to make ends meet. This had a huge impact on Jim. In one of the more inspiring quotes from his talk, Jim shares…

"You can fail at what you don't want, so you might as well take a chance on doing what you love."

Read that one more time.

Now read it again.

Are you really stuck, or just choosing to ignore your calling?

Are you taking a chance on doing what you love?

Be honest. If you are, YES!!!!! There is nothing that feels better than walking in the direction that speaks to your heart and authenticity. Regardless of the success you feel on this path it will always get you out of bed in the morning motivated and ready to go.

If you are not, YES!!!! Now is the time. Now is the moment. Here. Now. What is one thing you can do today that is true and authentic to living and being the person you yearn to be? There are no small steps, just non-steps. Look in the direction you desire to go and take one baby step (or giant leap) today!

Hopefully I am modeling this for you as best I can. As I finish this book I have now been on my own professionally for less than a year. I walked away from a good job with great opportunities in order to follow my passion and purpose. I am not taking with me a list of clients or freelance work. I have no book deal. I have no nest egg to fall back on.

Is this scary? Absolutely!

But WOW...am I excited and having fun! In the short time since leaving my job I have begun authoring my life based on what I "want" to do instead of being stuck in "hoping" for things to come my way.

Yes, and…!

I still get to perform as an improvisational comedian and I love it. Every time I am on stage it serves as a reminder that life is meant to be lived in complete collaboration with the present moment. Nothing else matters. Yes, the future is important, but it is the presence you bring to the "now" that impacts tomorrow. Don't sell your life short today for what you fear might happen next week. Odds are those fears will never come to be, and even if they do you will be able to "yes, and" those as well.

That's it. It's your life.

Are you ready to "Live Yes, And?"

Acknowledgements

I'll be honest. I rarely read the acknowledgements in books. It is like eavesdropping on a private party of family and friends, none of whom I probably know. So, if you can relate to that feeling, don't feel obligated to keep reading. But, if you are curious to know more about the people who have tolerated my life in order to make this book available, read on. Trust me, they are a special group of people.

There is no way I am screwing up this first acknowledgement. First and foremost I need to thank my brilliant and gorgeous wife Hollister. Yes, I put brilliant before gorgeous. Because although I was first struck by her beauty in college that was so out of my league, it was her depth of soul and spiritual grace that allowed and continues to allow her radiance to shine. Her unconditional love for me is the only reason I am able to write this book. Her unwavering support and love has kept me buoyant during all of the times I felt I was failing as a husband and father. She is my biggest cheerleader, and the greatest "and" to my "yes."

I guess at this point I need to mention my children. Seriously, how devastated would they be once they eventually read this book (if ever) to see that I left them out of the acknowledgements. They will surely be taking care of me in the not so distant future, so I better make sure I don't burn those bridges now.

Trinity has never been a "daddy's girl." Honestly, that makes me proud. She lives with an independent strength beyond what I could ever teach her, to the extent that I am never afraid for her safety or well-being. I talk about living "yes," but she lives it. She has rightfully earned the nickname "All In Trin!" My oldest son Holland connects me to my heart in ways I cannot access easily on my own. When I talk about authenticity, I picture Holland. He cannot help but to exude every fiber of feeling and love he shares for the world. I would not have the empathy I feel today without his constant example. My youngest son Shepherd is the strength and resilience I never demonstrated as a child. Despite his age, his courage in the face of fear and adversity has inspired me to be bigger and bolder in my own self-confidence. My wife and I always joke, and truly believe, that our children chose our family. I am eternally grateful to be the recipient of their daily gifts and share the place they call home.

Simply put, my parents loved me. In addition to supplying me with everything I needed (and then some), they instilled in me the permission and inspiration to follow my heart and dreams. They couldn't have given me a greater gift. While some people spend a lifetime seeking to earn the approval of their parents, I received it unconditionally. The selflessness and compassion of my mom has rightfully earned her the nickname "St. June." I only hope she sees the courage and strength I have always seen. My dad earned the nickname through my childhood as the "Original B.A.!" Yes, he embraces his inner Bad Ass! Yet despite his heightened testosterone he was always a loving and tender influence in times of need. Much of his influence was unspoken, but always felt. My parents created and nurtured a safe environment for me to step into my "Yes, And!" As the youngest of four children, I looked up to my siblings. My sense of humor was inspired by my oldest sister Tiffiny. We have become great friends despite her early loathing of my existence, and I am blessed to have her brilliant creativity expressed in the logo for "Live Yes, And." My other sister Tammy has always been an example of quiet strength. She is a dedicated hard-worker that exemplifies principle, while always wearing a smile on her face. It beams in my thought even as I write this. Hmmmm. I feel like I am forgetting someone. Who is my third sibling? Oh yeah. My older brother Tiger. That guy. In all seriousness, in addition to reading through an early version of this book and giving great feedback, he has been the person I have admired most my whole life. True, he did a great job of ignoring me for the better part of my first 16 years, but that was just his way of playing hard to get. I have yet to meet a finer person than my big brother, and he has been a constant source of stability and support as I bang and stumble my way through life. That said, he was a bit of a jerk to me at times when I was younger, and I will never forget the time when I caught him in the mirror in our bathroom flexing his muscles while singing "Macho

Man!" I think he was 14 years old, but for the sake of this story, let's say he was in his 20's! I think we can finally say we're even.

Beyond family there are so many friends that have become family. I notice that these acknowledgements will be longer than the book if I don't cap my appreciation somehow. So, let's do this! Thank you Norm and Chet at the *Improv Asylum* for giving me my start! And, thank you Frank and Jesse for being my "yes, and" brothers on and off stage for the past 11+ years with *The JOVE Improv*. Thank you Chris Raymond for being the best boss ever and showing me what a real "yes, and" corporate team looks like. Thank you Traci Fenton for letting me be a part of your world changing work with *WorldBlu* - and for always encouraging me to be bigger than I thought I could be. Thank you Quiet Lightening for taking me under your wing and being my friend and mentor as I entered the leadership and coaching space. Your work with *Educare* is immeasurable, and you know you have an assistant coach whenever you need one. I need to thank AG and SP for being my soul sister's. Your support for me (and my whole AT fam) is all over this book. We will forever hang in the OFF Lounge. Thank you Courtney for designing my web site and capturing my spirit. Thank you to the eternally sweet and talented Cristina for capturing the book cover perfectly. You know the two of us will work together for many more projects to come. Kari (or Karu), you were the perfect fit for proofreading this book. You get me and the whole Thomas gang, and I am so grateful you jumped in to make this more special. Thank you Carol Hohle for always being such a wonderful friend with a professional eye for all of my projects. Thank you for helping me get this labor of love to the finish line. Evan Griffith - my book publishing pioneer! Everyone needs a friend like Evan. Although I doubt myself all of the time, you make me feel there is nothing I can't do. It is wonderfully sickening how positive and inspiring you are. Here are too many more creative retreats and weekly breakfast "yes, and" boosts!

The tipping point in writing this book came in January 2015. I just got word I that I would not be jumping on a plane to speak to the US Men's National Soccer Team as I had been told. I was too down to go to work so I decided to sulk at Starbucks. It was there that I met my literary guardian angel. Philip Jarrett is the father of one of the IMG students I worked with regularly. The only open seat in the coffee shop was next to him. He and I had never spoke much, but as I shared my frustrating morning he told me how much he appreciated the work I did with his son. In fact, he told me that I needed to write a book. And that was it. That was the tipping point. So thank you Philip for being the perfect message at the perfect time. And look, you even made it into the book!

Of course there are so many more people that need to be thanked, and I am sure you will remind me who you are once you see that you didn't make it in. My e-mail address is still the same, so I look forward to hearing from you!

About the Author

Travis Thomas is the creator of *Live Yes, And* where he inspires individuals, teams, and companies to discover their inner brilliance through a commitment to purpose, authenticity, and life-transforming collaboration. He has shared his message with audiences all over the United States in corporate trainings, workshops, conferences, and as a one-on-one performance specialist. For over 2 years he served as a leadership consultant at IMG Academy in Florida where he trained and motivated professional, collegiate, and youth athletes from all over the world. He is the creator of *30 Days of YES* and he is the host of *The Weekly Yes, And Podcast*. When not on the road sharing his message he recharges in Jupiter, FL with his wife and three kids (and land shark dog). He is the creator of *RAK Friday* and he encourages all of you to change the world through random acts of kindness! You can also find him performing multiple times a month as a co-founding member of *The Jove Comedy*.

Find our more about Travis at www.LiveYesAnd.com and follow him on social media at @LiveYesAnd

Made in the USA
Lexington, KY
29 June 2018